THE A.A.U. WASTELAND

by Dave Taylor and Eli Gonzalez

Chapter 1

A CALL IN THE NIGHT

The call woke me at midnight. It was an hour I had learned brought mostly bad news. I had been coaching talent-rich youth basketball players on an AAU team that was in contention for that summer's title. Many of my teenage players were from rough Northern California neighborhoods, and their lives reflected their daily struggles. On that particular night, my dreams about on-the-court aspects of coaching, the X's and O's of offense and defense, had been interrupted. Deep in my heart, I knew that this call likely involved one of my off-the-court responsibilities, the kind of responsibility that, unfortunately, not all coaches shared because they carried the most mental anguish. I felt that one of my kids might be in trouble and I was going to have to get out of my comfort zone to be of help.

I flicked on a lamp and watched my hand tremble slightly as I reached for my phone, "Coach Taylor," I said, realizing how exhausted and vulnerable my own voice sounded. "Who's this?"

I didn't immediately identify the male's voice. Then, below what sounded like raw, uncontrolled sobbing, I heard a whisper.

"It's me, Coach. It's Rashawn Bell."

"Rashawn Bell," I muttered in sync with him. Somehow I knew it would be the seventeen-year-old African American youth from the inner city of Oakland.

"Coach, I need you," he said with soft desperation. "Can you come get me? My dad is trying to kill me."

"Give me your address," I told him in my calmest tone. "I'll be there in forty-five minutes. Stay tight, but if you need to call 911, don't hesitate."

"Please, Coach. No cops." His voice sounded guarded, and I pictured him speaking into a cupped palm as he recited his address. "My dad's been drinking, and I gotta get out of here." A sob escaped him, and I felt it shoot straight into my heart. "Can you come help me? Please, Coach Taylor, I don't know what to do."

"Hold on, Rashawn," I said. "I'm on my way."

I phoned Jason Hitt, my assistant coach. He answered after two rings with, "Yeah," as if he too shared telepathy about our young team members' chaotic lifestyles.

"Trouble with Rashawn's father," I told him. "Get your shoes on, oh, and grab your baseball bat." I wasn't kidding and he knew it.

"I'm out the door in five," he said in a clear voice, "at your house in fifteen."

Jason and I spoke in the shorthand most longtime friends are able to master. Together, on the job, just a shared look conveyed so much about the swift strategy and precise execution needed for success in what we do.

Rashawn Bell was the victim of a broken home. His mom had trouble holding a job and his father had recently been released from jail. Rashawn, though, had displayed NBA talent. However, this could work the wrong way coming so early in a kid's life. The youth had been singled out and showered with promises of fame and fortune. Oddly enough, his individual persona, though based primarily on his potential at this point, had begun to supersede what was once his father's reign over his household.

Whatever my kid's troubles would prove to be, the thought of him in jeopardy had set the game clock in my head beating toward a buzzer blast that signaled the end of a game.

*

I aimed my Sebring convertible toward Oakland, fabric top up to help keep us anonymous on that warm night. Two friends in shorts, t-shirts, battered sneakers, and unshaven faces who were determined to stick our noses into a fight between a young boy who played basketball as if he was born for the sport and a father who was having a difficult time adjusting to his own freedom. Down the line, would Rashawn repeat his father's mistakes? Could we make a difference and break the chain? We were just basketball coaches. It was a gamble and I hated the odds, but I kept driving.

Jason continued trying to contact Rashawn on the phone. "Any luck?" I asked.

"He's whispering," Jason said.

"And?"

"We need to hurry."

I accelerated the vehicle.

"Don't blow the top off, Dave."

"I'm barely over the speed limit."

"You're driving fifteen miles per hour over the speed limit," he said, as he made sure his seatbelt was on right.

"Are we there yet?"

He chuckled, "Not yet, but we're rapidly approaching."

I slowed down when I saw the rows of apartment complexes take shape ahead, and my throat went dry. I was once again entering the hood just like a real-life White Shadow!

I managed to catch some addresses along Rashawn's block. There were no other movements on the darkened streets besides ours, which was always a good sign.

"Here's the place," I said, my voice low as a burglar's. "Bring that folder of papers."

"Got'em," Jason said. "How about the baseball bat?"

For some reason, this struck me as pathetically funny. "Leave it. We're the peace makers." Getting out of the car, I looked right and left. We had parked in the heart of Oakland's most disadvantaged section of town. All was quiet. I led the way up to the stoop of the small apartment. Before I raised a fist to knock, my top player opened the door and stood in its frame, tears streaming down his cheeks. Six foot three and fast, this kid could have left me in my tracks and dunked a basketball before I could blink. Typically, I saw him in his alpha-male role but, on that night, he slowly walked outside and cowered behind Jason. His mother immediately replaced him, her figure not as tall as her son's, but more imposing. It was not lost on me that Rashawn's father would be huge.

"Coach Taylor," she said, her voice a breathless warning. "Please come in."

I stood inside and positioned myself non-threateningly in front of Mr. Bell, who now stood before me. I measured in at 6'8" and 215 pounds and I was confident, after checking his eyes, that the man facing me was not contemplating a full-out confrontation. But he was drunk and I didn't trust drunks.

"Sir," I began in my most authoritative voice, "I just want to make sure you're aware that I know what's going on here. I've seen this before and this whole thing can be turned around. No need to get further upset." I pivoted to Jason and then back to Mr. Bell, who was every bit as large as I suspected. "This is my assistant Jason Hitt, sir, and he's going to leave our contact information with you and Rashawn's mother."

Thankfully, Mr. Bell seemed to have given up any notion of raising Hell. I helped him sit at the kitchen table. Rashawn and his mother refused my gesture for them to sit as well. Jason opened our folder in front of them.

"Take your time in going over this, Mrs. Bell," he said.

After counting a minute off the game clock in my head, I placed a hand on Mrs. Bell's upper arm. "Read this carefully, read it twice if you have to," I said. "Once you are sure you understand, tell me if you agree with the terms I've written out." I looked into Rashawn's wet eyes, unsure of the legality of my actions, before looking again at his mother for another sixty clicks. "Mrs. Bell, you understand that if you sign this, you will be giving me the authority to make decisions for your son. It also protects me from any possible kidnapping charge that you or his father may try to levy against me in the future."

She took my pen and signed the paper against her hip so fast that I heard Jason gasp behind me.

"Thank you." She appeared to be relieved and heartbroken at the same time, "Take him someplace safe." She embraced Rashawn so hard that his breath escaped him. "Take good care of him, Coach Taylor. Please take care of my boy."

*

My adrenaline pumped the entire way back to my place. I questioned if I might have acted irresponsibly. *Had I done the right thing?* Rashawn sat next to me in the back while Jason drove at exactly the legal speed limit. When we passed a lit area, I saw Rashawn's facial muscles tremble; his cheeks were glistened with tears.

I didn't want to ask, but I had to know, "Your mom going to be okay?"

"Yeah," he said, "My dad's problems are with me, not with her."

I didn't push him for more. He covered his face with his large hands, suffering what I suspected was a combination of embarrassment, desperation, fear, and exhaustion. As we moved along in the darkness, Jason and I got fragments of what we had both heard before from kids like Rashawn. His father, fresh out of jail, was on a drinking binge. He started yelling at Rashawn and when his son, no longer the little boy, didn't look scared, he used his hands to strike him and toss him around. In an attempt to protect himself and de-escalate the situation, Rashawn was forced to seek solace in a small closet while his father roared, "My son has everything and I have nothing!"

I asked again, "Should we have called the police?"

"No," Rashawn said.

"We'll call your mom as soon as we get back," Jason told him. "We'll call her daily."

"Several times a day," I added, checking Rashawn's cheeks to see if he'd stopped crying.

We didn't say much more on the rest of the drive. When we parked in front of my place and got out of my Sebring, Jason fist bumped Rashawn's knuckles and shot me a concerned look that silently asked: *What in hell have we just done?*

"I'll call you in the morning," I said, then realized it *was* morning. The nightmare had taken five hours.

Inside my house, I set Rashawn up in my spare bedroom.

"Get some rest," I told him, knowing it was best not to over-talk these types of situations at the time. "I want you to call your mom after you get some rest."

"I will, Coach."

When I put my arm around his sturdy shoulders, I saw a young man determined to break his father's hold on him. I thought back to when Jason and I had barged into his apartment, probably the second or third cramped space he had lived in during his young life. Had I seen evidence of brothers, sisters, anyone else in the Bell household? No, but I would have bet there were other siblings. Maybe an older brother or sister who'd lost too many chances and had left the fold for the streets. Perhaps there was a younger child in the house who idolized Rashawn for his work ethic and determination to better himself. He or she would be left to wonder why he was no longer there. Who would help if their father did the same to them?

I called to him, "All settled in there, big guy?"

"All settled, Coach."

Sitting on the edge of my bed, I tried to wind down but had all sorts of unanswerable questions zinging through my mind. What high school will take him for his senior year? Will we find the money he'll need? Can I adopt him? Should I adopt him? Will it be possible for him to play for me while he's living here in my place? Are there going to be violations regarding NCAA eligibility? If so, who can I appeal to in order that he is legally able to play anywhere without breaking NCAA restrictions?

This may sound exaggerated to you. That a mother would give a summer league coach the authority to take her son and, for the foreseeable future, make decisions for him; big decisions too, such as where to go to High School and which college to attend! The AAU world seems to operate on a different set of parenting rules though. This is actually quite common.

WELCOME TO AAU BASKETBALL

Rashawn Bell's case is not an isolated one. There are thousands of kids who can attest to having similar tragic lives. I lied flat on my back and played videos of kids I had coached over the years in my head. As the dim light of dawn filled the room, I listened for any sound from Rashawn, for any small noise out of him that spoke of suffering. This would not be the only time I took a player in and became his legal guardian; it would happen twice more through my days as a coach.

MY NAME IS DAVE TAYLOR, AND I'M A BASKETBALL ADDICT

I love the game of basketball so much that I made it my livelihood to coach it at the grassroots level. When people see the enthusiasm and energy I coach or run my basketball camps with, I often get asked: "Why is it that you love basketball the way you do?"

I usually hold them hostage for twenty minutes as I explain my addiction of basketball, but I'll try to give you the short answer:

I love the athletic and intellectual challenge. It's a game that requires you to play on both ends of the floor. Although it's a team game, there is a mano-a-mano duel that goes on at every position. It's the only major sport where you can say, "Okay, you scored on me, but can you stop me from scoring on you?" In baseball, the batters face a pitcher but don't get to pitch to that pitcher. In football, if you're on offense and someone lays you out, you can't come back onto the field to play defense and get a chance to knock that same guy to the ground. In hockey, a player goes against a goalie to score but that goalie can't go at the player to score on him. Also, it's not boxing or mixed martial arts where it's a total man to man battle because Dr. Naismith's game is a team game.

In my opinion, the game of basketball requires athleticism and split second thought that can only be described as instinctual. You have to use your hands and your feet. You have to have finesse and touch while playing through contact with power. For most of the game, you are on the move more than the other "big-league" team sports. It's a game of individual skills fitting within a team concept. It's a graceful, powerful, aggressive, and intellectual game. When you see a team gel on defense, talking to one another, helping each other out, anticipating what the offense is going to do, switching defenders, trapping, boxing out, and getting the stop it's a beautiful thing! The only thing that's just as pretty in sports is watching a well-coached offense share the ball, identify the mismatches, isolate the hot-hand, set solid screens, swing the ball around, and find a deadly sharpshooter for an open shot; I tell you, that's visible poetry right there. Yes, that was the short answer.

Eli, my co-writer, says it's important for me to tell you who I am before I tell you what I have to say. He says it will carry more weight when I discuss the fundamental problems that have spread over the grassroots basketball program like a cancer, so as Jay-Z so eloquently put it, "Allow me to introduce myself." I crack myself up!

I coached Division I basketball at the United States Air Force Academy for four years and I was also a head varsity basketball coach at the high school level in California for fifteen years. I have been coaching high profile AAU teams and running camps with exceptional talent for over twenty years. I have been involved with the Double Pump AAU organization for decades. I have run the ADIDAS Jr. Phenom Camp since it started over ten years ago. I have been involved with the West Coast All-Star camp basically from its inception. I have helped run dozens of NCAA certified events, including the Adidas Superstar Camp in Georgia and numerous tournaments such as the Best of Summer tournament in Anaheim, California. I also work with NBA players when I run their camps nationally. Shortly, I'll also be working the Plumlee Big Man camps. I have also gone to Tokyo to run basketball skills camps and will be heading to Australia, Beijing, and Singapore, as well as other countries to teach and coach the game of basketball. However, I primarily concentrate on running youth skill and fundamental development camps for kids up to the age of eighteen. I feel this is the most rewarding experience I have. Having worked with college players and NBA players, I find that kids from ages twelve to eighteen are in the most need of guidance and mentorship. They can be influenced in a positive way which can impact their lives for future success. That is why I concentrate on that age group more than others.

When Eli asked me to mention players I have worked with before they went to college and wound up in the NBA, I honestly had to shorten the list so I didn't bore you. Working as many camps as I have, working as many tournaments as I have, and assisting with or running as many high level AAU teams as I have, the list is far too long and will likely consist of players the average fan has never heard of. However, since he is so insistent, here are some of the players I have either coached or had in my camps: James Hardin, Carlos Boozer, Paul George, Clay Thompson, Drue Holiday, Trevor Ariza, Agent Zero – Gilbert Arenas, Mike Dunleavey Jr., Michael Beasley, John Wall, Michael Kidd Gilchrest, Derrick Favors, and the Lopez twins just to name a few. I have met hundreds of D-1 coaches in the country as well as countless NBA and college scouts. I am a character in and was a source of information for the New York Times best-seller *Play their Hearts Out* and I'm in the basketball documentary Hoop Dreams 2.

I say all of that to reiterate that I love basketball and have great experience in this sport. However, there is a dark reality in the game I love that I alluded to earlier and it is killing this great game. There is such an infusion of corruption, wealth, irresponsible coaches, highly volatile and ignorant parents, and sensationalism that it is ripping the game away from good coaches and caretakers of the game.

I see thousands of young boys with their hoop dreams getting destroyed by hoop reality. Many of these kids never recover. This is a world where the bad guys often win and the good guys often lose. It's a world where dishonest guys with money use kids for their own benefit and they win while honest, hardworking coaches who take the time to cultivate a raw recruit into something special and pour their time and philosophies about basketball and life into these kids lose. Big shoe companies such as Nike, Adidas, and Reebok, as well as athletic apparel companies like Under Armour, have a lot more say in where a kid goes to play college basketball than the general public knows. It's sickening.

Something has to change. Someone has to stand up. As I go through the process to write this and realize how deeply rooted the problems are, I feel as though I am spitting into the eye of a storm. Still, someone has to stand up and Hell, it may as well be me.

Enter the world of grassroots basketball with me. I can't promise that you're going to like what you see though. I intend to pull the rug up to show you the hidden mess that this system has become. It's called Hoops Reality.

CHAPTER 2

WHAT YOUTH BASKETBALL SHOULD BE AND WHAT YOUTH BASKETBALL IS

T his is what a youth sports programs should do:

- <u>Teach young people the value of working hard:</u> It's called practice! They should learn that by working hard for something, it will pay off.
- <u>Teach responsibility:</u> Teach them to show up on time for practices and games and to keep their uniform in decent shape (typically the moms handle that but I know plenty of kids who pride themselves in taking care of their own gear).

- <u>Teach young people how to play with others:</u> Doing this will ensure that, when they are older, they have a better balance and are emotionally and intellectually better prepared to succeed in a work environment.
- <u>Instill a healthy respect for competition:</u> Teach them how to deal with winning and losing to better prepare them for the challenges of life.
- <u>Teach Sportsmanship:</u> Teach them how to handle winning graciously and how to lose with class and dignity. They also need to learn to play fair and respect others.
- <u>Teach Social Skills:</u> Teach them that by playing with and getting to know others outside of their circle, how to belong to a like-minded group of people, and how to work together for a common goal.
- <u>Give each child a healthy dose of self-esteem:</u> They should feel like athletes, winners, go-getters, and competitors. Self-esteem is said to come from the mind, body, and the soul; team sports help in each of those areas.

However, what high-level youth basketball is doing right now is:

- Preparing kids for failure.

Thousands of talented kids ranging from twelve to eighteen years old are being told by irresponsible coaches, teachers, parents, peers, and scouts they are on a trajectory to make it to the NBA. Only sixty make it on a team.

So, you have thousands of eighteen years olds that are told they are going to make it to the NBA by someone who wants them to play for their team. They are treated deferentially. They are given money, sneakers, more money, gear, and little responsibilities along with this self-destructing prophecy. All of their teenager years, when most kids are hitting the books, they're hitting the hardwood and someone else is handling the books. When Hoop Reality hits them and they don't even get a scholarship to one of the top seventy-five ranked schools, the "wake up" from their Hoop Dream is ugly...sad and ugly.

It isn't the kids' fault. They trusted people put in places of trust and believed what they were told. Now, the player has a poor education, his spirits are irreparably crushed, he doesn't dare trust anyone again, and is set free to impact society. Way to go AAU! (Please note the dripping sarcasm.)

IT'S NOT SOCIETY'S PROBLEM, BUT IT IS

When describing the problems in the sport of basketball, I think you have to use a broad stroke within your mind. The problems in basketball are not unique to that of the entire youth sports industry. In fact, the problems within professional basketball are the same as problems within youth basketball and are the same as problems within society. These problems exist because the world of basketball is a microcosm of society in general and draws many

parallels. I feel it is important that I lay a premise to my explanation for what the problems are in basketball.

In my humble opinion, society in this country has taken a turn
for the worst in the last five to ten years. Ironically, this directly
parallels with the downfall of youth basketball and youth sports in
general. We have too much political correctness and it has ruined
this country! That's right, I said it. We have become a country
where, if someone does not like the way things are going, whether
they are at work, school, or sport, we play the blame game. What
happened to out-working your coworkers? What happened to not
watching TV or playing video games the night before a test and
actually studying? What happened to admitting that we need to
quit complaining and actually do what the coach is asking you to
do? Instead we complain about our boss, a teacher, or a coach and
blame them for ruining our lives. PahLease!

Where is the good ole American toughness that built this
country? The type of toughness where we put our heads down
and got to work, we figured it out. Is that old-fashioned?

Our ultra-touchy society has forgotten the strengths of our
forefathers. Instead, we are twenty years deep in learning how to
deal with adversity from the great role models in reality shows
like Jersey Shore, The Real World, Bad Girls Club, or one of the
fifty "Housewives" shows. The ironic thing is that I'm talking
about parents here!

Is there such a thing as being too politically correct? There is when it means we've become soft. When the right person doesn't get a job because of filling up a quota, when a coach gets fired for standing up for the rules he established in the beginning and having principles, when all a student has to say is a teacher did something wrong and the teacher gets suspended or fired without any proof...then yes, there is such a thing as too much politically correctness. I don't see it as good thing.

To see how far we have gone as a society, the top four searches on Google on February 5, 2014 are the following:

1. Racing to save the stray dogs of Sochi.
2. George Zimmerman wants to box DMX but no deal made yet.
3. A sports story of three time world champion Curt Schilling and his new unfortunate battle with cancer. (I'm rooting for you big guy, Go Curt!)
4. When Tom Sizemore said that Elizabeth Hurley had engaged in a year-long affair with Bill Clinton, he was deep in his drug addiction, so it shouldn't count.

Does anyone else see a major fall from grace in our society? These are our top four searches on the most popular search engine! We worry more about who is married to whom and let our own marriages crumble. leaving millions of kids without a mother or father. Then, to compensate, the remaining parent babies them to the point that our schooling is slipping, our jobs are being outsourced, our prisons are bursting at the seams, and our dollar is losing its value. Our society, YOU AND ME, we are part of the problem. Because youth basketball is not played on Mars, the good and bad of our society infiltrate our game.

> "Discipline is the bridge between goals and accomplishments"
>
> Jim Rohn: Entrepreneur, Author and Motivational Speaker

LET'S TALK TEAM AND DISCIPLINE

One of the greatest moments in my life was having private discussions with Coach Wooden at his residence. He had always been my role model and to be able to go to his condo and sit with him for hours, on several occasions, is one of the greatest highlights of my life. During one conversation, I asked him what the most important thing in developing a winning team was. Coach Wooden's response to my question was, "team". He went on to explain that the team must be together, must be unified, and must play as one! He said that the team must have discipline and mental toughness to execute under diverse conditions. It is the coach's responsibility to provide these lessons and values in practice. He made it very clear that there had to be rules and consequences that the coach provides in order for success both on and off the court! His entire philosophy was based on making his players better people so that when they graduated from college, they were ready for society and prepared to better themselves and their community. A coach who could not instill discipline could not be a good coach. To this day, I still apply many of the teachings Coach Wooden imparted on me in my coaching conversations with him.

It saddens me to admit it, but this style of coach would not last long in today's society. In Coach Wooden's Pyramid of Success, which details values, victory, and peace of mind, the Pyramid has five levels. On the base we have the following categories:

1) Industriousness. There is no substitute for hard work.

2) Friendship. For friendship to exist, it requires a joint effort.

3) Loyalty. Be loyal to yourself and to all those depending on you.

4) Cooperation. Be interested in finding the best way, not in having your own way.

5) Enthusiasm. You must truly enjoy what you are doing.

Second Level:

1) Self-Control. Practice self-discipline and keep emotions under control.

2) Alertness. Be observant and eager to learn and improve.

3) Initiative. Do not be afraid of failure, but learn from it.

4) Intentness. Be determined and persistent.

Third level:

1) Condition. Mental, moral, and physical moderation must be practiced.

2) Skill. A knowledge of and the ability to execute the fundamentals.

3) Team Spirit. An eagerness to sacrifice personal interest for the welfare of all.

Fourth Level:

1) Poise. Just be yourself.

2) Confidence. Be prepared and keep proper perspective.

Fifth Level – the peak of the pyramid:

1) Competitive Greatness. Be at your best when your best is needed!

Two other topics of major importance to Coach Wooden are Faith and Patience, which are dying breeds judging by today's standards.

This is a great explanation of what each and every coach should be instilling in each and every child they have in their circle of influence. But, in today's society, we may never see the likes of a John Wooden again. I would advise every coach to pattern their coaching style after Coach Wooden's Pyramid of Success.

SWEET BEARD DUDE

One example of Coach Wooden's discipline is a well-documented story of when he had one of the greatest college players in the history of basketball playing for him. His name was Bill Walton. Coach Wooden had a rule on his team and it was not necessarily a basketball rule, it was a "personal conduct" or private rule that he had as a coach. This rule was no facial hair. Well, after one of Walton's greatest years on the court where he led his team to a National Championship and was named player of the year, he went away for the summer. It is well known that Bill Walton was a product of the '60's. He was a "hippie" so to speak and, when he came back to school and was preparing for his first day of practice, he had a beard that would rival that of ZZ Top! He approached Coach Wooden and said how he had rights and there were people fighting a war in Vietnam to protect those rights and he felt that, as an American citizen, it was his right to have a beard. Now, I assume that Walton felt there was no way Coach Wooden would not allow him to do whatever he wanted because, in Walton's mind and just about everyone else's, he was the best player in the world and without him, UCLA would lose. He knew that Coach Wooden needed him in order to win. So, Coach Wooden pondered what his young player just said and replied with great joy. He went on to tell his player how proud he was of Walton, how proud he was because he had a belief so strong that he made a decision and took a stand. That is what Coach Wooden wanted, to develop players that had the intestinal fortitude to take a stand in something they believed in. He was beaming with pride. Walton must have smiled so big, saying in his head, "YES! I knew he would do whatever I said because I am the man! Not only am I his best player, I'm the best player in all of college basketball."

It must have come as a massive shock when Coach Wooden followed with, "I am proud of you William, and we will miss you this year!" The look he gave Walton was that of absoluteness. He was not joking; he had practice starting in fifteen minutes and he needed to prepare for practice with or without Walton. Bill Walton then sprinted into the bathroom and shaved that beard in five minutes! The process of shaving that size of beard in that amount of time must have been painful but he did it and arrived at practice on time.

Could you imagine a coach doing that today? If a coach tried to instill **pre-set rules** today, players would transfer. The player and/or parent would file litigation or the player would run to the principal and school board saying that the coach was prejudiced against him and if the principal did not make the coach change his rule, the parent would not only sue the coach, but the school, the principal, the school district, and anyone else affiliated with the program. I say this because it has happened.

SCHOOL BOARD, "SHE STAYS ON THE TEAM!"

I know of a coach that cut a player because she missed too many practices and games. She was not a good teammate and brought the team's spirits down. She was good, but felt that she was above doing what all of her teammates were required to do. So, the coach had private meetings where he expressed his displeasure and stated that if she did not pick it up, she was going to be cut. She agreed and clearly understood the consequences. However, she continued to behave in the same manner. So naturally, the coach cut her! She then told her parents, which led to a complaint to the principal. The principal backed the coach, which was rare when discussing a star player. The parents then went to the school district and school board saying how unfair it was. The parents made a couple threats and next thing you know, the coach was told that he had to keep her on the team!

Once the coach heard this, much to his credit, he resigned. To him, I want to say congratulations for having so much integrity that it was more important to you than your status as a coach. The system lost another good coach but you simply can't continue to coach a team of boys or girls effectively when your credibility has been diluted. Cases like this often make me wonder if administrators care about anything other than wins and losses and pleasing nonsensical parents for fear of possible litigation.

Too often there are no winners in grassroots basketball.

CHAPTER 3

GET TO KNOW ME

I was a gym rat. As a kid, I'd play basketball alone or with others until the streetlights came on. At night, I'd watch the sport until our TV went to Carson, Letterman, or silver-haired evangelists. I lived for basketball. When I wasn't on the hardwood or asphalt, I carried my ball wherever I went. The sphere of inflated leather became part of my portraiture. My most valuable life lessons came to me through practicing and playing the game. Immersed in the sport, I found a way to deal with failure while capturing degrees of success. I set goals, bettered my skills, learned to persevere, and learned to never give up. If you've ever witnessed a kid find himself through an activity, you know what I'm talking about.

"I'm going to put myself through college with an athletic scholarship," I told my parents after my first year playing varsity for North High School in Torrance.

"You're already over six feet four and next year you'll be only a sophomore," my mother said. "You could be another Magic Johnson."

"I'm afraid you're going to have to get that athletic or academic scholarship though," my father said. "Your mom and I will do all we can to help you, but ..."

He didn't need to say more.

Wanting to be more than just a big kid destined to hang around under the basket, I pushed myself in practice to prove my value on the full court. I realized that, although I had height, I lacked the strength required of a major college post player. With that in mind, I decided that I needed to focus on being a guard. I knew if I could develop my guard skills and get recruited as a guard, my size would be advantageous and my lack of strength would be less of a deterrent. My greatest on court role model would lead my way. His name was Magic Johnson.

I went after what I wanted, vowing to never let anyone tell me what I couldn't do. My behavior improved. I stayed out of trouble and focused on improving my grades. When other kids my age were smoking, drinking, and experimenting with drugs, I refrained. Without an impeccable scholastic record, I knew that playing at the next level would never amount to anything more than a dream. Basketball kept me clean, kept me focused, and kept me smart. I began to think I needed the game to breathe, let alone exist with pride. During my teen years, when many of my friends became listless, I rushed forward in my size thirteen Converse to compete. Yeah, I wanted it, just as much or more than thousands of other high school kids back in those days.

Even in my down time I would watch *The White Shadow* television series, starring Ken Howard as Coach Ken Reeves. The tall, blond actor had enough game to handle a dozen inner city kids. Coach Ken Reeves was a badass.

Then, the opportunity came. I was good enough to qualify for a scholarship. There was just one problem: I didn't have an SAT score. Why? Because I had never taken an SAT test. I didn't even know what an SAT was!

My teachers went into emergency mode. I took the test, sweated it out, and learned my score. I knew so little about it that I repeated only my math score to a college coach that had asked how I did. That's how close I came to washing out before I even started. I remember there was a long silence.

"Well, it's not high enough to qualify you, not for the Air Force Academy."

"There's another number here too. Let me see... for English." I read the score. It was one of the highest. I had qualified and then some. I still remember how proud my mother was.

I knew that the hard work was just the beginning. This was not going to be a free ride in a Division II college. It was a military school, but that was what I wanted. I craved the structure and the challenge. Sure, I felt the fear, but I had put constant pressure on myself since I was thirteen years old. I ate fear up!

"I can handle it," I promised my mother and myself.

I pictured myself having a college career like Magic Johnson or Larry Bird, then becoming a coach like the White Shadow. I wanted that interaction between a coach and his team. That would be my mission. I ended up playing for the Air Force Falcons without coming near the fame of Johnson's or Bird's. After my playing career was over, I focused on the next challenge: coaching!

DAVE TAYLOR TURNS INTO COACH TAYLOR

I remember how well I thought I would be able to relate to the players when I first started coaching. After all, I had just passed through the process they were on. For example, if I told a kid to put extra work in, I could tell him that I had to do the same. I had no idea how helpful going through the process would be and still is today.

I thought again of the fictional coach in *The White Shadow*. I never missed an episode growing up and I loved how Coach Reeves always managed to win in the end. He wasn't just a coach, he was a mentor and a teacher and his players learned more from him than from their "real" teachers. Sure, the series depicted real life situations, but the scripts always came to satisfying endings. The kid who was threatening the coach's life realized the error of his ways, the dirty cop framing the star player tried a move that backfired, or the mother who believed Reeves was unfair to her son discovered how the coach's plan was molding him into a champion.

The reality of the AAU system and grassroots basketball in general is that there are no writers that script the end results. There are no directors to yell out "Cut!" once a scene has passed a certain point of tension or violence. The kid doesn't always see the error of his ways and he inevitably takes his talent down a dark alley and never reemerges full of promise.

Who regulates the system anyway? I'm talking about the high school level AAU system. Whose job is it to make sure that amateur athletes are protected, treated fairly, and not taken advantage of? Is it the job of the NBA? Can it be the job of the NCAA?

Each college only recruits a handful of players a year at best. Why should they be responsible for the millions of kids that won't even go to their schools? Maybe it should be the high schools. But many AAU leagues are played throughout the summer and the schools have no jurisdiction over kids during the summer. Hmmm...who does that leave? Quite frankly, it doesn't leave anybody! Unbeknownst to even the rabid college and NBA fans, there are millions of dollars being spent and made at the grassroots level. Yes, I said millions! Yet, no one is policing it. The "Play Fair" committee hasn't set up shop yet. Besides, once they do, how would they enforce the rules?

A COACH'S CONVERSATION WITH HIS ASSISTANT

"Isn't that right?"

Jason Hitt gave me a look from the driver's seat. We were leaving the scene of a crime. The crime was our AAU Team California losing in overtime to a group we should have beaten like a drum. "I smell it too, Dave," he said.

I breathed deeply, "I smell corruption." We had lost to a team that obviously had illegal players on their roster. I knew some of the players and they were two years older than the legal age. Some players played for other teams and were recruited for this game. This team had so many illegal players that it was bordering on a felony! I'd begun to suspect the game I'd adored for decades was becoming a heartless system wherein AAU and high school basketball seemed to issue the stink of rot. How could I to claim such a thing? I'd been around this hardwood universe for a long time and I'd begun to observe behaviors through the various programs that made me cringe.

"We're losing," he said, watching the gymnasium disappear in his rearview mirror, "and I don't mean just this game today." He meant us, the so-called good guys.

"This fun loving machine we call youth basketball has finally become a full grown monster." That must had been the hundredth time I'd said that this week alone. I was preaching to the choir.

Jason snorted, "A beast." He checked the speedometer to make sure he was driving the speed limit. "The sad thing is, I doubt your average sports fan knows anything about it."

He was right about that. Yet, thousands paid sufficient money to watch teenage athletes, both male and female, play in front of the most rabid of audiences one could imagine. This truly American sport was slipping away from us. Europe was catching up fast. Why were we falling behind? Much of the blame lay at the feet of the AAU, an organization that seemed determined to continuously display its incompetence and poor judgment.

"Remember Rashawn Bell? I asked. "All I have to do is think about Rashawn and all the kids who could be his clone—or could be his exact opposite. Sometimes you can't tell. The kids before Rashawn and the kids who'll arrive from neighborhoods in opposite sections of town. They all will be strolling in to sign up next season with one thing on their minds." Speaking of Rashawn, he was fortunate. He went on to play Division I basketball, went on to play in the NBA, and went on to play overseas. I couldn't help but wonder how many other kids were out there like him but did not have a coach to help them escape their negative situation. It made me feel good believing that Jason and I played a small part in the eventual success of Rashawn. But how many more needed us?

Jason picked up on my thought. "They all think they're the best prospect to ever walk into a gym!"

"How do we tell them that they have some work to do, that they will have to earn their minutes on the floor?" I knew I sounded like a broken record, but I kept rolling. "In this day of parents and outside mentors developing websites and chat forums to hype their kids and promote them as an agent would a client, will coaches like us be able to mold them into even passable teammates?"

"Not easy," Jason agreed, "not when most of them have their own entourages posting blogs about them on social media forums, Facebook pages, and YouTube clips. The worst thing is that these kids believe their own hype!"

"It's time we start speaking the truth. It's time we all be honest and not worry about being politically correct or not. I'm going to speak from my heart about my kids." We drove in silence for a bit, the buildings moving past us looking more desolate by the city block. "Nothing changes," I said. "Everything changes."

"Right," Jason said, probably just to pacify me.

"We have parents working as agents. We see posts on social media that would have put an asshole blogger in jail just a few years ago. We got nine-year-old kids posting three-minute highlight clips."

"It's insane," Jason said.

"Shall I save the parents for later?"

"Yeah," Jason said. "Let's get back to the real culprits."

"The shoe companies..."

"I was thinking the AAU."

"Who do you think runs the AAU?" This was the rhetorical question that had been echoing in my head for too long.

He turned into my driveway and sighed, "What would John Wooden do?" he asked.

Later that night, I thought John Wooden would blow the top off of grassroots basketball. He would write a book.

Chapter

THE PLAYERS

PLAYERS RUN THE SHOW

$\mathbb{L}$et's face it, kids today have it easy, even if they won't admit it. They've never had to walk uphill for three miles in an arctic blizzard and then have to walk again for three miles in the same blizzard to get home. It's a different age for kids today. At the age of six, they stop believing in Santa. Forget Santa, they're playing video games rated M for Mature! The flow of information today is more rampant than ever. Naturally, it is going to breed a different type of teenager or, in this case, a different type of athlete.

Social media sites such as YouTube and Facebook have become sites where young kids with talent get sensationalized to the point that it causes their psyche some ill effects. Players today come to their freshman year of high school basketball with major scars, delusional dreams, and incredible baggage. Let me fill you in on what happens to good, young players and how it has allowed the lunatics to run the asylum.

This is the path that many highly athletic sixth graders go through. We're going to name this prototypical player "Adam." This is Adam's life:

In the fourth grade, Adam is the leading scorer in his intramural league. Unbeknownst to him, a few "scouts" have come to see if he has "the right stuff." These scouts are coaches from some of the better AAU teams in the area and the right stuff is his overall size, shoe size, size of his parents, etc. They want to see if young Adam looks as if he might be well over six feet. Then they look at his athletic ability above all else. They look for a play or two to wow them. Ideally, they would like a player to make the type of play that people will pay to see and a player they can hype. They don't bother to look at where Adam lives because they have become adept at working around that situation. Heck, they'll raise him for a while if he's good enough!

After the game they approach Adam and tell him how good he is. Adam smiles sheepishly, but he loves it. They tell Adam that they are with Program X, and tell Adam a few of the kids that have played there or that are currently playing there. Adam sobers up a bit and his little face crinkles up, trying to appear focused. He's already overwhelmed.

"Why don't you come see one of our games next week? I can pick you, your mom, and your dad up and we can watch the game and I'll take you guys out to eat. It'll be so much fun. What do you think?"

They'll tell Adam's parents, "Your boy has got some serious talent."

"Oh, thank you, that's nice of you to say that. That's all he wants to do," Adams mother says. "He loves basketball"

They look her in the eye and say, "Now, I'm not sure if you understand, but I've been working with kids his age all the way up to college and if you do the right things with Adam, he could make the NBA!"

Adam's mother laughs only to realize that they are serious. Dead Serious.

"The NBA? No way, I mean, how can you tell, he's only eleven!"

The unofficial scout will name-drop players they worked with who went on to the NBA when they were eleven. Of course, it might not be the truth, but that's not the objective. The objective is to get Adam to play for their team.

On the ride home, Adam's parents tell him that they think he has the right stuff to go the NBA, if he takes it seriously. Adam decides to take it serious. Just like that, the game Adam loved is now his significant other. From this point on, his life will change in ways he could never expect to keep her happy, to hear her seductively whisper to him, "You're going to make it to the NBA baby."

Adam works on his dribbling and on his hops like a madman. He stops taking the bus to school and dribbles the ball to and from school. His parents start to ask if he's going to go out to practice. They used to ask if he did his homework. Adam's friends are amazed at his ball handling skills.

"You need to put up a video kid," Adam's friend tells him.

Adam keeps doing the two handed dribbling drill with two balls. He puts one in between his legs then the other and repeats it a little faster each time, as if he's a little basketball cyborg. It takes quite a few takes and edits but, eventually, Adam has a two minute clip of handling the ball in a way that Bob Cousy never knew it could be handled. The video goes viral and Adam's world is never the same.

First, all of the other kids at his school see it, then they show it to their friends, who share it with....oh, you know how a video goes viral, right? Well, before you know it, young Adam is a celebrity and everyone is whispering that he's going to the NBA!

Adam starts with his traveling team right about the time he gets to the sixth grade. He doesn't play with the friends he grew up with as much; he has to play with the best players if he's going to make it to the NBA. He's very attentive to his first "real" coach, who tells the young team that he's not going to sugarcoat things. He is going to talk to them like grown men because it's a big bad world out there and the sooner they realize it, the better off they'll be. Remember, Adam is only eleven going on twelve.

Adam plays in his first game and the kid has talent. He plays well, he dazzles with his dribbling and shooting, but he doesn't look up when he has the ball and plays little to no defense. That's okay though, the behind the back-between the legs dribble to split the defense is all anyone remembered anyway. They don't realize he is bigger, faster, stronger, and more mature than most of his peers in the sixth grade!

His next practice, he comes in ten minutes late. Coach had waited for him to arrive to start practice; it's inconceivable to start practice without Adam! The thing is, Adam didn't come alone, he has what can only be called an entourage. Someone had driven him to practice who his coach and/or parents don't know. There are also a few other people that don't look like stand-up citizens and two cute young females to round out the group.

The coach talks to Adam with his "real talk" language and Adam hangs his head in obedience. He apologizes to his coach and they get to practice. After practice, one of Adam's new friends tells him he shouldn't take that crap from that coach.

"Who the hell does he think he is? People don't go to see him coach, they come to see you playa. They come to see what Adam gone' do"

"Yeah, he ain't got no two hundred thousand views on his video," says another crony.

The season wears on and Adam is a sight to see with the ball. His speed and quickness with the ball is a beauty to watch for a kid his age. No one asks where that speed or athleticism is on defense because this is the AAU. No one plays defense. It's Show Case U! At least, that's what his coach had told him once during a one-on-one chat.

The next year, Adam comes in with an even bigger entourage. But now his mother is the ringleader. She has to protect her investment, I mean, baby boy, because he's going to make it to the NBA. Adam soon becomes a ranked player. That's right, Adam is currently ranked twenty-first out of all sixth graders in the country and, out of them, he is ranked the third best point guard.

They rank players in middle school. Can you imagine the pressure that puts on a kid? But I digress, let's get back to Adam. But, before we do, I need to repeat that for you – they rank players in MIDDLE SCHOOL!

Adam gets home schooled so that he can repeat the seventh grade. His AAU coach convinces his mother that if he plays against people a year younger, he will look more dominant in his games. So, Adam goes through the seventh grade twice, without really learning anything once. In the eighth grade, he switches a couple of times to different teams because suddenly, "Coach don't know how to coach someone with my talent." He gets to the incredibly daunting task reaching high school as a celebrity. His home games are sold out, he's in the newspaper after every game, and soon, his away games are sold out because everyone heard that one day Adam will be in the NBA and they all want to have a "I knew that kid back when...." story.

"Adam, you need to pick up your grades if you want to go to college," his high school guidance counselor tells him. She loves him. He's so charismatic.

"My teachers suck. They can't teach. I don't understand them," Adam says. "Besides, why do I have to know math when I'm in the NBA, I'll have accountants for that."

She laughs, "But without the right grades, big schools won't take a chance on you and then how will you get to the NBA?" She has him and she knows it. He'll do the right thing; this kid has everything going for him.

"I'll just go play in Europe for a year."

Little does Adam know, someone talked to his most recently trusted AAU coach, who tells him that the school he's playing at is not visible enough. They talk to his mother and tell her that if he wants to impress real D-1 or NBA scouts, he needs to play on a bigger stage against better talent. Adam's mother says she can't just 'up and move' her whole family. Mr. AAU Coach tells her she doesn't have to. He'll watch over Adam during the week. Adam can go home on weekends and he'll still be on the road to the NBA.

Now, Adam is living with someone he's only known for three months, going to a new school, and is expected to be the next Michael Jordan. Adam is in his junior year and he's playing against the top kids in the area. No one on his new team likes him; he's a selfish ball-hog and they haven't spent any time with him.

For the first time, Adam starts to struggle on the court. The kids he plays against are bigger, stronger, and faster than he was used to. They aren't in awe of him or his five hundred thousand view video; they have videos of their own. He still plays terrible defense and now his teammates are holding him responsible for it. His new coach though, he's an "Adam guy." Someone made a promise to him and he's going to cash in on it by helping Adam if it kills him (Adam) or not. Now his teammates hate him even more because he's the coach's pet. Adam complains to his surrogate dad/AAU coach.

"They're just jealous of you, Adam. Life is going to bring haters and you just have to learn how to deal with them. You go out there on that court and you do you, don't worry about your team." Great advice, dad.

Adam calls his mother, who was already coached on what to say by his surrogate dad. "So what do you want to do baby, come back here and have no future? You just have to be tough. We'll all look back and laugh about this when you're in the NBA!"

Adam is scared to tell people that, for the first time, he's not sure he can make it to the NBA. His life starts to resemble a lie. Meanwhile, his last game was a 13 point, 1 assist, 5 turnover game. Not the stuff of legends.

Adam is alone in the middle of his entourage. If they see the cracks, they're not telling. They aren't going to abandon their lottery ticket. Adam stops doing his schoolwork but, that's okay, because his "tutor" does it for him. He really stopped going to school to learn sometime in seventh grade which means, no matter how old he gets, he might only be as smart as a seventh grader. Adam pushes away his teachers, his coach, and his AAU coach/surrogate dad.

When he starts his senior year, his playing time is shortened for a kid who transferred from another school who everyone says is a lock to make it to the NBA. The newspaper photographer only seems to take pictures of this new kid. Adam hates him, and his team hates him too.

THE END OF ADAM'S STORY

His AAU coach/surrogate father sends him back to his mother's house immediately after the high school season. He had to transfer back for the last couple of months but this time, without his tutor. Somehow he graduates high school (a sign of how our educational system is broken but I will save that tale for my second book). Then it's all downhill from there. Without a scholarship things get bad at home. He can't believe his mother would let him live with that guy they had just met and his mother can't believe he ruined their chances of being rich. His younger siblings, who used to look up to him, now see him as the screw-up. No one buys him anything anymore. No one picks him up when he needs a ride. He's too prideful to get a job. Fast-forward five years and Adam is society's problem. He has no skills so in his words he begins, "doing what I gotta do" to make money. He's in and out of jail until finally he goes back in and doesn't come out.

THERE ARE TOO MANY ADAMS TO COUNT

I have personally seen more Adams than I care to admit. In the last fifteen years, players have become less mature and less developed, yet more entitled. These kids have been enabled for much of their young lives and, therefore, have lost the level of learning ability that is required of a child.

Here is what happens: A kid goes to a camp in the fifth grade and plays well, it just so happens to be a camp where there are scouts and a ranking is attained. They then become known as a Top Thirty player for their age group and, with that, comes a bit of notoriety. With that notoriety, depending on the parent, it could lead to a sense of entitlement. The kid actually starts to hear the hype and, in most cases, believe it. It is ridiculous to me that a twelve to fifteen year old would have "hype" surrounding their skills.

The child, at that age, is under developed and immature. They may grow another foot in height; they may not grow another inch! They may find academic difficulties, find trouble with the law, find a girlfriend, and/or lose focus. There are a myriad of complications that can arise from the ages of twelve to eighteen. I find these years to be the most important in a person's development with regards to character and personality. I have no problem saying that, for his age group, at this particular time, he is an above average player. I have no problem with camps where the best players at these age groups compete. However, ranking them does a massive disservice to good young players.

There is not an organization today that can accurately rank every kid at that age anyway, so ranking them is, at the very least, grossly irresponsible. It does so much harm to kids that it should be illegal.

More often than not, ranking players at that age is a detriment to their development because they are not capable of dealing with the pressures that come with such a label and they are not mature enough to understand that the label means absolutely nothing! With this new sense of entitlement, they decide to stop working. They stop developing their skills; they live off their laurels. They think they are already one of the best so why would they work more? This is the beginning of the end and why rankings usually mean the decline of the player.

These players start to feel "special," as if the rules do not apply to them. Therefore, they are increasingly more difficult to coach. This "superstar" player will challenge the coach, break rules, or lack the effort at times of the average player. It is the coach's responsibility to remedy that attitude. The problem is, the coach fears such actions will lead to the player becoming unhappy and transferring. So, the coach's ultimate desire to win will be stronger than his desire to do right by the player, to educate and lead. So, rather than discipline the player, he will enable the player. This will demonstrate to the player that he is not to be held responsible for his actions. Instead, said player follows a different set of rules. Because he never taught the player how to accept criticism and be better for it, he never learns how to deal with criticism, which is otherwise known as coaching, and this will hinder the player's development both on and off the court.

The high school rules allowing players to transfer at the drop of a hat has played a major role in the decline of talent and the increase in poor play. Back in the day, you had to attend the school that you were assigned based on where you resided. Now, any player can go anywhere and that has scared coaches more than anything. Coaches are so afraid of a talented player transferring that the coach will very rarely discipline the player. This leads to poor chemistry, poor play, and poor attitudes. I do not know how these coaches can look in the mirror after having players dictate the coach's behavior. This even bleeds into the collegiate level.

The players have been given too much power. I remember when it was nearly impossible for a player to transfer and equally difficult for a coach to retract a scholarship. Watch that movie *One on One* for an example. Allowing a player to leave for any reason and attend any school he wants leads to major problems at the high school level. Coaches recruit, parents negotiate, and players dictate. These are major issues. These are children still living in their formative years. They need to be educated. Instead, they hold all the cards and never learn the life lessons that come with participating in a disciplined program.

It's not just the fear of a kid transferring that has coaches scared, that's just one of the on-court situations. There is a more serious fear coaches live with. This is the fear of the player on a personal level. Players today are not stupid. They know the political climate we live in now. I have had coaches tell me stories that scared me to the point of almost quitting my job.

"I'LL SAY HE HIT ME"

A player can say whatever they want and the school will always listen.

I had a coaching friend of mine who is a lot like me tell me one day that a player came to him and said, "If you do not play me, I will tell the principal that you hit me!"

Instances of coaches being falsely accused are way more prevalent in high school than in AAU; after all, there is no one to complain to in AAU! This particular coach was also a teacher at the school. An accusation could not only cost him his coaching job but his teaching career. A scandal like that could ensure that he never even teach at another school again. He was facing losing his livelihood, all for a player who felt he should have gotten more playing time. This coach stuck to his guns and pretty much said a la Clint Eastwood, "Go ahead; make my day."

The kid went through with it and told his parents, who then reported him to the athletic director and the principal. The school did an "investigation" and concluded that the coach was innocent. However, his reputation had taken a hit and he saw the writing on the wall.

"All it would take is another selfish kid and then how would I provide for my family?"

He was a disciplinarian type of a coach, one who would tell the kids how to act and, if they didn't act appropriately, he made them face the consequences. He never cut the player on the "advice" of the school committee, but the kid got less playing time than before. However, he admitted to me that at times he was fearful of another accusation. The coach resigned after that season and still teaches at that high school today. The kid in question tried to get on a junior college team but never made it. I never heard of him again.

SOME PLAYERS TODAY ARE SMART. NOT GOOD SMART, BAD SMART

Players today know that an allegation alone would damage a coach's reputation so much that it could destroy his career. It's surprising what someone will do if they think another person stands in the way of them making millions of dollars. Unfortunately, that's the reality of the high school and AAU systems. So many kids have been told that they have a shot at the

NBA and, if they find themselves in a system that doesn't show-case their talent or if they're not playing enough, some would do or say whatever it takes! I once heard of a parent that attempted to sue a coach for being detrimental to the family making millions of dollars. Can you believe that? A parent actually took a coach to court over playing time in youth basketball. Thankfully, the ridiculous case was thrown out.

It's not just false accusations that gives players power. At times, it can be their entourage, gang members, or family members. Coaches are often viewed as "bad guys" to the hanger-ons of talented players if the player starts to struggle. Although it doesn't happen often, coaches have been assaulted and physically hurt for not yielding to a player's demand. Damage to physical property such as their house or car is also an occurrence. Once a coach caves, other players follow suit. It's ugly, but this is the reality at some high schools.

A kid knows that, even if an accusation is found untrue, he can say something happened and it becomes a matter of hearsay in which the coach has no defense. To make things worse, the administrations these days would rather relieve a coach than stand by him in the midst of a scandal. Players today know this and they use it. They are the stars and, if they're not treated as such, heads are going to roll. Their parents said so!

LEBRON, DURANT, OR BATTIER?

Selfishness is a cancer that's slowly spreading from the NBA down to grassroots basketball. The NBA does a better job of show-casing Lebron James vs. Kevin Durant more than the Cleveland Caveliers vs. the Oklahoma City Thunder. So, naturally, every kid wants to be like Lebron or Durant. Before I go any further, please know that I respect Lebron and Durant and think they are the best players in the game. I'm not criticizing them, I'm criticizing the NBA marketing machine and how each kid wants to be "The Man" on their team. No one wants to be the glue guy. No one wants to play like a Shane Battier. Ever hear of him?

Shane won the Mr. Basketball award in 1997.

He played four years at Duke, although he could have left early for the NBA.

He led Duke to a 2001 National Championship.

In 2001, he won the major National Player of the Year Award.

He is the only player to have ever won both the Naismith Prep Player of the Year Award (1997) and the Naismith College Player of the Year Award (2001).

He was the sixth overall pick of the 2001 NBA draft.

He has played for the Grizzlies (twice), Houston Rockets, and Miami Heat.

During the 2012-2013 regular season, Battier and the Heat won twenty-seven consecutive games, establishing the NBA's second-longest winning streak. A speech given by Battier following the Super Bowl has been credited with sparking the streak.

He has won an Olympic Gold Medal

He scored 18 points on 6 of 8 3-point field goals in an intense game 7 against the Spurs to win his second NBA Championship.

But nobody wants to be Shane Battier? Nope, he's not on Sports Center enough. Despite all of his accolades, kids today feel that Shane doesn't have enough swag or enough street cred.

AAU teams are comprised of top players. The problem is that these top players don't pass like the LeBron's or Durant's. They just care about their stats and their personal swag. It's a shame when kids today label players like Battier as soft. He guards the other team's best scorer night in and night out and he's soft? He didn't get swayed by the lure of the NBA until he finished college and he's soft? I'll tell you the real reason why they don't want to be like a Shane Battier:

He's not selfish enough.

How sad is that?

ISIAH THOMAS AT INDIANA

I'd like to put a disclaimer on this story. It was told to me by several third party sources. Therefore, I can't say it happened unequivocally. I trust the people that told me and I hope it's true because I'd like to believe in players like this.

I was told that when Isiah Thomas was playing at the University of Indiana for the Hall of Fame coach Bobby Knight, there was a rule that if you were late, regardless of the reason, you would not play. So, one day while on his way to practice with his girlfriend, they got a flat tire about four miles from the gym. He had about forty five minutes until practice started. He got out of the car, walked around to the passenger side where his girlfriend was sitting and surely expecting to see her boyfriend preparing to put on the spare. Instead of grabbing a spare, he opened her door, gave her a kiss on the cheek, and said, "Sorry babe, I have practice soon and we have Michigan State tomorrow and I can't be late!" He proceeded to run to practice, leaving her to deal with the flat tire.

Now, whether or not this story is true, it should serve as inspiration. There are still kids like that today. There are plenty of kids who have survived the perils of notoriety either because of their faith or good parenting or they have seen too much poverty and heartbreak and know they need to be the ones to effect change for themselves and their families. I love those types of players. Yes, I have to do more for my "knuckle head" players out of necessity, but those dedicated players are my favorite to coach and I root for them with everything I have.

THE PUSSY STORY

(I will not name names or the schools associated with this story because of the respect I still hold for some people at these schools.) I attended an all-star high level event hosted by a major shoe company. The cost for the event was upwards of $750,000 to host which was chump change for the shoe company. They held a "seminar" for high school kids with elite talent at a hall that seated 300 people.

As with every seminar, there were special keynote speakers. At this particular event, we had lined up several Division I players that were a lock to make it to the NBA, barring any major injuries, to talk about the college life. The intent was to motivate and educate the high school kids about the perils and pitfalls of the college life as a student athlete. These "speakers" were instructed to tell the kids that they were going to have to work hard to balance basketball, practice, the spotlight, managing their time, class work, obligations, and everything else that was going to be thrown their way. Four major universities were represented by players. I'm talking about programs that have a legitimate shot to win a national championship any given year.

The first college player/speaker went up to the podium to a hushed silence. The high school kids knew that, in less than a year, he would be playing in the NBA. He walked up to the podium with a confident strut. He was used to attention; his confidence was hypnotic to the room. Before even opening up his mouth he had the room in his hands.

"You want to know what college basketball is like?" he asked before pausing. "The best part about college basketball, what I will remember the most..." you could hear a pin drop, "the pussy," he said with a wide grin.

The room exploded as the hundreds of high school sophomores, juniors, and seniors jumped out of their seat as if they were at a Def Jam Comedy show. He continued, "No, hold up, hold up," he said with his hands up to get their attention, "I'm not talking about regular pussy, I'm talking about fine ass pussy!" The more he mentioned that word, the louder and more obnoxious the kids got.

I felt as if I walked into a bizarre dream. This couldn't be happening at such a big-time event in front of the assembled alumni, scouts, and coaches. Oh, and did I mention that most of the high school kids were there with their parents? It was humiliating for the school. He was there as a representative of a nationally respected program! We expected to hear about "the struggle" and how it was worth it for the sake of the championship or to one day make it to the NBA.

The next player/speaker approached the podium to a different room now. The laughter and exuberance of youth was still bouncing off the walls. Instead of bringing the seminar back to a semblance of respectability, he continued where his predecessor left off.

"What about classes?" a high school junior asked. "Do you pick your own classes or do the coaches pick them for you, and is it hard to stay on top of your classes with all the travel?" My growing anger subsided a bit. Here we go. Here comes the realistic view of academic life and the struggle of managing their time in college. Nope.

"Whatchu talking about classes for?" was the answer. "Man, aint nobody care about school. You don't even have to go to class! The coaches take care of all that. I wouldn't even worry about school bra, real talk."

I had to leave the room. What was happening to the game I gave my life for made me want to yell and cry at the same time. Obviously, the coaches who weren't present were informed of the actions of their players. Years later, during a conversation with the now NBA bench player who had said the infamous remarks, he told me that his coach never even mentioned the incident. A few years after, that coach and one of the players involved won a national championship. One of the players that played a key role on their championship run attended that particular event as a high school student. Maybe he went to that university based on the description of a college basketball player's life. Or, it could have been that his father got hired to the coaching staff when he arrived.

This is how some elite players live from the ages of fifteen to sixteen: without consequences and with the world handed to them. And you wonder why the NBA has the problems they have.

I guarantee you a player from a Bobby Knight led team, a Tom Izzo led team, or a Coach K. led team would not have behaved in this manner! This is why we need certain college teams to succeed. They do things the right way! I recently attended a Duke game and sat behind the bench. At one particular time, a player was taken out of the game and he looked at the coach, ready to argue and explain why he should not have been taken out when he caught himself. He stopped in mid excuse and simply said, "My bad coach, I'm wrong." He knew if he continued to debate his removal from the game, he might not get back in. This was a highly touted freshman and it was great to see.

The bottom line is this: In the AAU System, the players hold the power today, but it's the bad coaches who gave it to them.

CHAPTER 5

THE COACH

WHAT IS A COACH?

I did a search for the definition of the word "coach." I think it's important for anyone reading this to understand the term correctly. No, I'm not talking about a horse-drawn carriage and no, I'm not talking about an expensive handbag. Forgive me, my sarcasm gets the best of me from time to time. I'm talking about a person selected to lead a team or individual in a sporting contest.

Coach (as defined by the Merriam-Webster dictionary):

1. A person who teaches and trains an athlete or performer.
2. A person who teaches and trains the members of a sports team and makes decisions about how the team plays during games.

That's the bare bones description of a coach; unfortunately, there are far too many bare bones coaches out there. There are coaches, good coaches, and terrible coaches.

This is Dave Taylor's definition of a coach: An effective communicator who commands the attention and respect of his players because of his knowledge of the game, passion for the game, and concern for each player's welfare. A coach holds everyone equally accountable and, although he primarily teaches basketball, he also teaches a little about life.

"There is no greater compliment a person can call you, than COACH!" – John Wooden.

Unfortunately, in all of my years in the grassroots system, I have noted that good coaches as defined above are becoming a thing of the past and bad coaches are becoming the norm. I'll tell you some of the reasons why. There is just so much to say I don't know where to start!

So that we're on the same page, I'm mainly referring in this chapter to the High School/AAU level coach. You moms and dads who coach your third grade son's team, I have advice for you at the end of this book. However, I don't have the scope locked in on you; bless your hearts for taking time out of your day so that Junior can play his favorite sport. I hope you're teaching the fundamentals and a good work ethic, sportsmanship, team chemistry, and the life lessons of the game. At the third, fourth, and fifth grade level, basketball should be a lot more about those things.

At the sixth grade level, the winning gets to be a lot more important and it gets worse at every level after that. At the high school level it can get downright ugly. This is where I'm locked in with my phaser. I'm switching from Stun to Kill.

The main reason for the decline of the "good coach" is too much political correctness and I know I'm being politically incorrect in saying so. It has become increasingly difficult for a coach to manage the team in the optimum way of making the player individually better and the team collectively better. The problem is that we have way too many pansy ass players!

- They can't take constructive criticism.
- They all think they're Michael Jordan version 2.0.
- They whine that they don't play enough.

- They whine that they run too much in practice.
- They talk while the coach is talking, they dribble the ball while the coach is talking, and then they talk bad about the coach because coach always yells.
- They know the rules but break them and then they cry foul when consequence is doled out.
- They don't run the play and get upset when they're subbed out.

I'm going to stop there even though I can go on and on. Yes, I know I'm talking about the players and this is supposed to be about coaches. Patience, Daniel-san; before I talk about the coaches I wanted to inform you of what many coaches have to work with.

DISCIPLINE

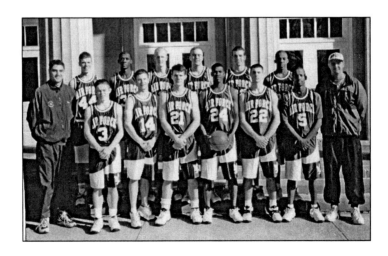

Discipline is the first thing that you need to instill in your players. Without discipline, all you have is anarchy. What was once considered a respected and admirable quality has taken the backseat in this generation that doesn't really know how to say no to anything. What we have ultimately become are a people that have forgotten how to sacrifice and work hard. We opt for the easy way out, the sexy, the here and now. This is because discipline is gone and we're only after what appeases and appeals to us in the moment.

Discipline is one of the most necessary traits for success.

As a coach, you have to consider that those players who opted to try out and compete to play for you have put themselves before you and it's up to you how they will behave. They don't want to be average. They want to be student-athletes. Being a student-athlete was cool back in the day, is still cool today, and will always be cool. (Although I'm not sure that the word cool is still cool today.) They will work for it if you know how to coach. They want to be part of your team. You have the power! You decide the rules!

Look, you're going to get challenged by players from time to time but don't you teach how to overcome challenges in the games? Teach Discipline. Preach Discipline. Uphold Discipline. Don't waver on Discipline. If you do all these things, guess what type of a program you're going to have? That's right: A disciplined program. I'm not talking about a dictatorship; I'm talking about a program with certain pre-set rules that are enforced if broken.

Dictators suck; don't be That Guy!

IT'S MORE ABOUT ME THAT IN IS ABOUT YOU!

A majority of coaches today fall into the selfish category. There are two types of coaches: Those that coach for the kids and those that coach for themselves. If you're coaching to build a resume so that you can get a better paying coaching gig, that's okay, I get that. We all want to improve and get better paying jobs. However, if you feel that you are judged solely by wins and losses, I hope you don't take that mentality to another program because you just don't get it.

Many today, coach for themselves. They believe that they only coach basketball and if a player does something outside of the gym, it's not their problem. If you're that type of coach, do yourself and the kids a favor, quit! Someone has entrusted you in a position of leadership and authority. The kids and their parents look to you for more help than just how to run a three man weave or how to break a full court press!

All these coaches care about is winning, which means they don't care about the players' development. To teach a kid that the only thing that matters is the end result is incredibly irresponsible. I'll repeat myself here because I want you to know what a bad coach is and I want a bad coach to know that he's a bad coach in the hopes that he will change. Bad coaches do not care about the player developing on and off the court!

DAVE TAYLOR'S SIGNS ON HOW TO SPOT A BAD COACH

They give their best players preferential treatment.

- They allow their best players to show up late, talk back, not go hard in practice, take plays off, and yell/embarrass teammates. If any coach treats any player by a set of easier or more lenient rules, that's a bad coach! If a coach can't demand more from his best player, he's a bad coach.

- Bill Russell had just won his first MVP trophy and the Celtics had just won another championship. When the next season started and the team attended their first practice, his coach Red Auerbach was all over him. He dogged him the entire practice. He knew that if the team saw that he could yell at the great Bill Russell, he could yell at anybody!

- Not knowing who their best player is.

- Your best player isn't always your highest scorer. It can be your lock-down defender. It can be the kid who says "nice shot" and gives a high-five to each teammate when they come off the court. He can be your Glue-Guy, the one that helps the individuals gel into a team from the inside.

- <u>They do not communicate effectively with their players and/or parents.</u>

  ○ Too many coaches don't tell the non-starters why they aren't starting. Even less coaches tell players that are at the very end of the rotation why they're at the end of their rotation. You have to be honest. If a kid is not playing, tell him why. Tell him what he needs to work on. Let him develop into a better player and not just seethe on the bench thinking you hate him. Tell the kid's parents why their kid isn't starting. It helps with the cohesiveness of your world as a coach when the kids and their parents know where they are with you and how to either keep their spot or take someone else's.

- <u>They flat-out don't know the game well enough.</u>

  ○ If all a mechanic knows is how to change a tire, it doesn't matter if he's wearing an oily one-piece mechanic suit and steel toe boots, that dude is not a mechanic! If you don't know the game you're coaching inside and out, you're not a coach, you're a Spot Holder. You're holding that spot until a real coach comes.

  ○ If your team is down by twenty in the first half and you're on your last time out, stop yelling at the kids for not playing hard, you did that on the first two timeouts. You need to be able to adjust your game plan! Switch to a zone. Send someone over to give the point guard a pick to get the ball up the court easier. Slow the game down. Speed the game up. In college, you can recruit the type of player that fits your coaching style. In high school, you get the players you get, (unless you recruit, which I think is unethical). You should be able to coach a variety of styles.

○ One of my pet peeves is to see a team losing and hear the coach berate the players without giving them any real help. Understand the game coach!

○ These coaches also don't have the guts to take responsibility for a loss. It's always someone else's fault. If you get out-coached, it's your fault. Learn to tell your team that you didn't adjust fast enough and you'll take this loss on you.

• <u>Coaches that don't better themselves in the off-season.</u>

○ Most coaches will tell their team what they need to improve on during the offseason, which is good. The bad thing is, the coach will not do anything to improve his/her skills! Go to a coaching clinic. Find out how successful programs are running their practices. Find a mentor!

○ I know of too many coaches that don't watch game film. "Hey, this isn't the pros!" they'll say. How about taking pride in your work and developing your coaching ability?

Then there are some coaches who will watch film but they'll bully-talk anyone else watching the film with them. Stop that! Watch film and be an observer, be a listener. Someone might see something you're missing but you've bullied them into not wanting to be there because you will belittle their comments.

- <u>They don't teach teamwork.</u>
  - ○ "Just give Billy the ball and the rest of you get out the way" is not a good play to run! You can have isolation plays in a team run play, but it goes deeper than that. You need to teach teamwork. Each member of the team is equally important. You're all Bulldogs or Eagles or Honey Badgers! Those players that don't play need to know that they push the starters in practice to make them better. They're still a valuable part of the team. Everyone on the team has a job to do and only when everyone does their job to the best of their abilities do you have a winning program regardless of the Win/Loss column.

- <u>Not enough balls.</u>
  - ○ I'm talking about those ball-hogging teams; what else did you think I meant? I have seen high school games that are just glorified pick-up games. There aren't enough basketballs on the court; everyone is just looking for their

shot. The game is played with one ball, learn to share it! If your best player/shooter is your point guard, that shouldn't mean that he dribbles up the court and shoots at will. Have him pass the ball, cut through the middle, sweep off to one side, and get the ball again – while he was doing all that, the team could pass it around three or four times. Now he gets the ball again at his preferred spot and everyone is involved. It's not rocket science.

○ Just because you're the best player doesn't mean you take the most shots! If you're getting double-teamed all game and you lead the team in field goal attempts, you don't know the game and neither does your coach! Plain and simple. If someone is double-teamed and the coach knows something called "spacing," someone is open! An open shot from a decent player is statistically a far superior shot to a tightly contested shot from a better player.

• <u>Being physically, verbally, or mentally abusive.</u>

○ You will see the top coaches in the NBA or College swear at their players and/or at the refs. After eighteen, you can sign up for the Armed Forces and fight and risk your lives for our country, so I think you can handle some profanity. However, middle school, high school, and AAU coaches... you're not coaching young adults, you're coaching kids. Yes, if a kid is sixteen years old he's is still a kid! If you can't refrain from using profanity in tense situations, how can you expect your players to handle tense situations on the court? The problem is, I know of some coaches who don't only use profanity during games, they'll use it at practice, on the team bus, and even on dinners with their players and their parents. When you become a coach, whenever you are with your team, you're always being viewed as their coach.

○ There is never a good reason to swear at a kid. Parents and school boards allow you to coach their children, not curse at them.

○ Mental abuse should be considered illegal. To play games with a kid's head is evil. Too many coaches try to teach certain kids a lesson and toy with them; these are horrible coaches. There is no excuse for you to publically embarrass a kid. Sure, there are times when you'll get a player who's too full of himself and you'll have to teach that player a lesson but that should be in your pre-set rules on behavior and the lesson should be to enforce the rules, not publically humiliate him in front of his peers.

○ Physical abuse is illegal! As a coach, you never have the right to snatch a kid up, grab him by the neck, kick them as they walk to the bench, or semi-punch their chests. I have seen coaches do this and more. How much is the game worth? Are you so enthralled in the competition that you become a bully to the kids who trust you?

- <u>Do It All Coaches.</u>
    - ○ Too many coaches want to do it all themselves. They'll have an assistant or a staff, yet they need to micro-manage every detail or do everything themselves. If you are one of those coaches, fire yourself, relax, and enjoy your life. Coaching is a team effort. Trust your staff. If you can't trust your staff, get a new one that you can trust. Tell your wife's brother's best friend's uncle that it's not working out and get someone who knows what they're doing.
    - ○ Bad coaches embarrass and berate their assistants. You're the top dog, the alpha male; they get it. You're the head coach...it says it on your shirt. Take a chill pill. There is no need to constantly demonstrate your authority by strip-ping your staff of theirs. Soon, the players won't respect them either and now your team is really headed in a bad direction.

The truth is that there are more DON'TS to coaching than I have here, but this is a good start.

IN EVERY GAME, THERE ARE TWO GAMES BEING PLAYED

In every sporting contest, there are two games being played: The game played on the court between the players and the game of strategy being played on the sidelines between the coaches. If the coach wins his battle, the odds are his players will win theirs.

My co-writer Eli Gonzalez coached a high school team before and he had a keen insight to this truth. Before his first game, he addressed his team and said, "I'm going against Coach Bill tonight and I know one thing, I'm gonna win my battle. If you execute, you'll win yours!"

He saw the faces of his players and you know what? They believed him! He was a first year coach but he had displayed all the attributes of a good coach. He knew the game and had molded the team into a functioning team. He out-strategized Coach Bill switching from zone to man and with what seemed like random full court presses. His players executed and played together and they both won.

This coach had two wins/loss columns. One was the win/ loss column that every team is graded on, the other was when he thought he either outcoached or got outcoached by the opposing coach. There were times when his team would win a game but he would put it as a loss in his column knowing that he got out-coached and vice versa. It looked a little like this:

Eagles	Coach
W	W
W	L
L	L
W	W
L	W

This is so true. Have you ever seen a perfectly called play but the player messes it up? Give that coach a W man, he deserves it. Unless of course, it's the right play but with the wrong personnel, but that's beside the point! J

LIVE BY EXAMPLE

At the end of the day, Coach, you're a role model whether you like it or not. If you're in a position of talking the talk, you need to walk the walk. I personally do not drink alcohol; I never have and never will. I also don't do drugs. I don't smoke, snort, or inject anything that I shouldn't. I understand that I'm in the minority. It's not illegal to drink alcohol, but that does not mean it is okay for you to get drunk while with your players. No player of mine will ever see me out of control, acting improperly, or being drunk. No player of yours should ever see you out of control, acting improperly, or being drunk either. You are a role model. You're their coach, not their buddy. They have enough buddies, but maybe only one coach. Take it seriously. If you can't abstain from drinking alcohol at a dinner when your team is with you, you might need help. For goodness' sake, drink after the dinner if you must.

COMPLAINERS SUCK

In life you'll meet a lot of complainers, too many if you ask me. Millions of people will look at any situation negatively and verbalize it. If you're a coach, you need to inject positivity into your players' lives. Someone has to be the optimist and guess what coach? That someone is you. I know it's not possible to always be positive, but at least try to be.

There is a scene in the movie *Saving Private Ryan* where Tom Hanks plays the role of Captain Miller. He and his squad are looking for Private Ryan. Edward Burns plays Private Reiben, one of the soldiers under Captain Miller's command. They all have an interesting dialogue on not only HOW to complain, but WHO to complain to! Private Reiben had been complaining for several scenes. Check out this conversation about complaining from Saving Private Ryan:

Private Jackson: Sir, I have an opinion on this matter.
Captain Miller: Well, by all means, share it with the squad.

Private Jackson: Well, from my way of thinking, sir, this entire mission is a serious misallocation of valuable military resources.

Captain Miller: Yeah. Go on.

Private Jackson: Well, it seems to me, sir, that God gave me a special gift, made me a fine instrument of warfare.

Captain Miller: Reiben, pay attention. Now, this is the way to gripe. Continue, Jackson.

Private Jackson: Well, what I mean by that, sir, is... if you was to put me and this here sniper rifle anywhere up to and including one mile of Adolf Hitler with a clear line of sight, sir... pack your bags, fellas, war's over. Amen.

Private Reiben: Oh, that's brilliant, bumpkin. Hey, so, Captain, what about you? I mean, you don't gripe at all?

Captain Miller: I don't gripe to *you*, Reiben. I'm a captain. There's a chain of command. Gripes go up, not down. Always up. You gripe to me, I gripe to my superior officer, so on, so on, and so on. I don't gripe to you. I don't gripe in front of you. You should know that as a Ranger.

Private Reiben: I'm sorry, sir, but uh... let's say you weren't a captain, or maybe I was a major. What would you say then?

Captain Miller: Well, in that case... I'd say, "This is an excellent mission, sir, with an extremely valuable objective, sir, worthy of my best efforts, sir. Moreover... I feel heartfelt sorrow for the mother of Private James Ryan and am willing to lay down my life and the lives of my men—especially you, Reiben—to ease her suffering."

Mellish: [chuckles] He's good.

Private Caparzo: I love him.

Captain Miller is always their Captain. They don't need to be in a battle for him to be Captain. You're always the Coach, even when you're not in a game or at practice. Gripes and complaints don't do any good if they go downward. Be positive. Teach your kids how to be positive and look for a solution instead of how to wallow in misery.

A coach needs to take their responsibilities seriously. At the end of the day, that's one of the things that differentiate a good coach from a bad one.

I have been blessed to be an assistant coach at the highest levels and learn from some of the greatest coaches out there. I have had some great mentors, especially at the college level. As a head coach, treat your assistants with respect and provide them with responsibilities. Delegate authority and give them a voice. Trust them. Let the team see that type of relationship, that type of teamwork.

If your influence and reach doesn't extend beyond the court, not only are you not doing your job, you don't know what your job is.

Chapter 6

AAU

WELCOME TO THE CIRCUS!

Have you ever been to a real circus like a Barnum & Bailey? The big-time circuses have three rings and, in each ring there is something incredible going on. AAU is exactly the same. It's a three ring circus. In one ring we have the players acting like prima-donnas, in the second ring we have parents totally freaking out and losing all civility, and in the third ring we have the sleazy scouts, greedy coaches, bribed refs, NBA players (past and present), and criminals. Somewhere up high with a megaphone are big shoe companies profiting from the chaos.

Have you ever seen the mess a circus leaves? There are feces from the elephants, horses, and other animals on the floor. There is also plenty of spilled popcorn, candy wrappers, and confetti. That mess is the loss of innocence of thousands of talented basketball playing kids.

AAU stands for Amateur Athletic Union. It sounds structured doesn't it? Amateur Athletic Union. It might not be very structured but, I tell you what, it's a multi-million dollar a year industry! Founded in 1888, the AAU's first goal was to represent American sports internationally. AAU teams blossomed in many sports and the organization became a driving force in preparing Olympic athletes. In 1978, the Amateur Sports Act established a governing body for American Olympic sports, usurping the AAU's role as an Olympic launching pad. Since then, the fundamentals and ethics have eroded from the AAU and it has become a money making machine that uses kids and spits them out for society to deal with them.

Before I go into the ills of the AAU system, if it can be called a system (it's more like the wild west of the 1800's), I want to make a note that I have met many wonderful people in the AAU. These are people that I consider friends. There are great teachers of the game and teachers of life that take time off of their day to coach AAU teams and they do a great job. I applaud them for their work and for keeping their hands clean in such a dirty organization.

Unfortunately, for every good person I meet in AAU, I seem to meet twenty bad ones. As a whole, the AAU system is extremely flawed. I assume the intent of the program was to assist the individual student athlete find better competition so that they could grow in the sport. Instead, what it has done is provide a blueprint for how not to behave in society; it has allowed corrupt individuals to get involved with impressionable kids and bring an underworld mentality to the great sport of basketball.

I also want to make clear that this chapter is mainly focused on the top sixty or so AAU programs in the country. So that you know, there are about twenty to thirty top-level programs within the AAU circuit, and then there are another twenty to thirty programs that are sniffing the top level. If you were to look at the ESPN Top 50 players year to year, they are involved in these national level powerhouse AAU programs. These, for the most part, are considered national programs, so I may not be talking about your local AAU team. Local high school city teams do a decent job, for the most part, and should be commended. I train and develop mostly top level talent, players that are a lock to make a Division I school and many players within that group that should make it to the NBA. So I'll stay there and talk about what I know.

There are many reasons why the rest of the world is catching up to us in basketball; some would say that the world has already caught up to us. Part of the reason is that the rest of the world has gotten better at teaching the fundamentals of the game. For this, I lay most of the blame on the Amateur Athletic Union, the AAU.

AMERICAN KIDS FLUNK BASKETBALL 101

There is a great *Wall Street Journal* article that I refer to at almost every camp I run. It features Michael Beasley, the second overall pick in the 2008 NBA draft. Michael is quoted as saying, "If you're playing defense in AAU, you don't need to be playing. I've honestly never seen anyone play defense in AAU."

Basketball can be broken down to two parts: offense and defense. Michael Beasley is right! You might think this is an exaggeration but I live there, I see it. Ole' style defense is not considered defense. You have incredibly athletic youngsters, I mean, the feats these kids can do is jaw-dropping; yet, with all their talents, they just go through the motions on defense and hog the ball on offense.

Former Orlando Magic Coach Stan Van Gundy had this to say: "It's a bad system for developing players. They aren't learning to handle the ball, and they aren't learning to make plays against pressure." (Again, because no one's playing defense.)

Coach Gundy also summed up the mentality he sees with the AAU so-called coaches: "If I can win the eleven to twelve year old league and tell all my friends about it, that is a whole lot more important than if my kids actually get any better or learn anything about the game."

In regards to European basketball, Mr. Van Gundy said: "Those guys are doing five or six practices for every game. They are spending a lot of time in the gym working on individual skills. It's reversed here."

Do yourself a favor and read the article. AAU has become a big money-maker and what little rules you would think they would have aren't enforced.

Not surprisingly, AAU officials declined to comment on the article.

Current Detroit Pistons player Brandon Jennings went to Europe for a year instead of college. He says he went the first two weeks without touching a basketball, they just ran. Then they practiced fundamentals and rarely scrimmaged. He says they were the most intense weeks of his basketball life. "If I would have never gone to Europe, I wouldn't know the pick-and-roll game. I wouldn't know how to guard and I wouldn't know how to fight through screens. I'm stronger now."

Mr. Jerry Colangelo, the national director of USA basketball who is in charge of the Olympic team, says the system is deeply flawed. He suggests giving high school coaches more access to their players, especially in the summer.

See? It's not just me!

HERE I GO WITH THE "COACHES" AGAIN

In my experience, the majority of these AAU coaches are severely underqualified. I am not saying that they have no knowledge; what I am saying is they are not qualified to coach the young student athlete between the ages of fifteen and eighteen. Those individuals need mentorship! They need to be schooled in character development, on and off the court. These young student athletes need to be sculpted and developed, not just in the fundamentals of basketball, but the fundamentals of life.

More often than not, these coaches are either coaching for a huge stipend or for notoriety, in hopes of one day piggy backing on the laurels of a great player and getting a college job. The AAU coach will make a "my player will go to your school if you hire me" type of agreement. It has been done more times than I can recall! But it's not only the coaches using these handshake negotiation tactics. Many of the parents use them as well. This happens all the time.

Okay, maybe not all the time, but more often than one would think. I'm talking about big time college programs giving well paying jobs to AAU coaches in order to get their player to play at their school! The Indiana Elite AAU team is under NCAA investigation as Eli and I write this book. According to an ESPN.com report, Drew Adams, the coach of AAU power Indiana Elite and his son recently got jobs under Indiana University Head Basketball Coach Tom Crean with no prior college coaching experience. After Drew was promoted to director of operations/video coordinator, Crean signed or picked up commitments from eight players with ties to A-Hope and/or the Indiana Elite Program. By the way, Drew Adams owns A-Hope, a non-profit foundation to try to help fulfill the dreams of young international players from Africa.

I'm not passing a verdict and I understand that many former students from Africa have gotten a college education from Drew's help through A-Hope, which is an incredibly awesome thing. But this is Indiana University we're talking about. The AAU world is a shady world full of side-deals and handshake deals and they're not like the good old-fashioned handshake deals that our forefathers used to do. These are handshake deals because they don't want to leave a paper trail!

WHAT DOES IT TAKE TO BE AN AAU COACH?

It's a complicated process (I'm joking of course). All you would have to do is take a ten-question True or False test. I believe you need to get seven out of ten correct. Then there's a background check. I don't know what they check for but, based on the sort of individuals that I've seen, I think the background check is just as rigorous as the True and False test.

Do you need prior coaching experience? Nope. Do you need to show any capacity for coaching? Nope. Communicating? Nope. How about a drug test? Nope. Anyone from parents to store clerks to gangsters can become a coach. A coach! Talk about devaluing a title. I know of coaches that have supposedly been discredited and banned from AAU participation, and yet... there they are coaching their team at their next game! It's not as if there is someone checking I.D.'s at the door. There are just far too many teams, too many participants, and too many tournaments for any governing body today to monitor.

So, the rules get violated constantly and there is no realistic solution to solving the problem with the exception of an absolute re-assembling of the entire process. I will explain later what MY solution would be to the problem.

ENTER THE CIRCUS...IF YOU DARE!

Walk into any high level AAU tournament that has been sanctioned by the NCAA as an observer of humanity. I dare you. It will change your life. There is an intense level of ineptitude that permeates at those venues. There are backroom deals being made, lives being threatened with physical violence, referee's either being threatened or bribed, and the parents?

Give me a television producer and a video camera and I'll give you a reality show hit! These parents are unbelievable. I'm talking a ratings bonanza unlike anything we have ever seen. Put it up against the Super Bowl and it would hold its own!

I'm not saying that the bulk of the parents aren't educated, have decent jobs, aren't sweet, kind, respectful and overall good standing citizens in our society. I'm sure most of them are. However, when their child, who has been prophesied to play in the NBA, suits up and plays an AAU game against other top level talent, any ounce of decorum they have just vacates the premises.

I have seen mild-mannered soccer moms who bake goodies to give away and attend PTA meetings channel their primitive instinct to protect their young and become raging lunatics! It is absolutely comical in the saddest kind of way. Parents at this level are far worse than any other level of sporting competition.

Next time you're in Vegas, LA, or NYC, forego the $100 theater shows; save your money and get buy a ticket to one of these games and you'll get more theater than you can handle.

DO YOU KNOW WHO I AM?

That's exactly what a former NBA player acting as an AAU coach said to me. This was in reaction to me asking him to put the required NCAA wristband on his wrist. Of course, he refused.

"Do you know who I am?" he asked, but it was more of a statement than a question.

"Yes, I do," I answered. "You're a coach and, as the coach of your team, the NCAA requires you to put this wristband on."

He exploded with profanity and then threatened me with physical violence. This was a multi-millionaire AAU coach. Some coaches that depend on the AAU to make a living are more aggressive than you can believe.

LOOK THIS UP!

Seriously, go online and do a search on this: On February 24, 2014, after the final whistle of a game of third graders, a coach of the Basketball Stars of New York Titans walked over to the stands and began punching a fan who apparently had been heckling him throughout the contest. The fan turned out to be a parent of one of the players who was on the losing side.

The organizer of the event is quoted as saying, "The parent was yelling shit across the court at him the whole game, I mean, who does that?"

Look it up. You'll see the ugly video of the incident.

Where do I begin with this one? Do I say how out of control and totally belligerent the parent was? Should I go after the coach for physically assaulting a spectator/parent? Should I say something about the knuckle head who organized the event for somehow excusing the coach's action? All three are idiots! You just can't argue with stupid. This was a third grade game! That makes these kids what, eight or nine years old?

At times, I just want to throw my hands up and say there's nothing that anyone can do to change it, but that's just not my style. That coach, who I saw on video assault a parent, might very well still be coaching his team today. Something has to change! Where's the outrage? Watch the violent video while it's still up.

The amount of scummy AAU coaches is exponential. I personally know over forty coaches that take their teams to Las Vegas for tournaments. When the clock hits midnight, they're at the strip clubs, gambling, partying, and getting into sophomoric trouble. I know because I'm there once a year for tournaments as well. If you walk around at 1:00 am, you will see hundreds of high school aged kids roaming the streets unsupervised! I don't know if it's okay with you to have your sixteen year old in Las Vegas at that time of night unsupervised, but it sure as hell isn't okay with me. There are bad people there; it's no wonder some coaches fit right in.

I once witnessed a former NBA player (a different one than in the previous story) physically attack a female site supervisor over a rules violation he was being called on. On his way out, he smashed the scoreboard! I would bet he's still coaching too.

WHY DO THESE PEOPLE COACH?

I can't speak for all of them, but many of the coaches I'm referring to do it to parlay their relationships into a life-changing deal. They recruit players that they hope to build strong relationships with so that, in a couple of years, they can get a nice payday for "encouraging" the player to a college program. The payday could be cash, cars, or jobs.

They also get paid quite handsomely by big shoe companies. It's not uncommon for a coach to get about $75,000 a year from a big shoe company along with $75,000 worth of merchandise to outfit his team. These coaches get paid by big shoe companies to start what's called "brand loyalty" with up and coming players. They are armed with cash and gifts to pay players to play for them. This is not a fairy tale. This is not a story about Big Foot or the Chupacabra. Have you ever heard of Hoop Dreams? Well, this is Hoops Reality in the AAU circuit.

Some players are offered everything from cash to cars to women to houses! It's much like the movie Blue Chips with one exception: There are no real rules and regulations deterring the AAU coach like there are with college or high school coaches. No one governs AAU!

I have been involved in programs where a parent would come up to say, "I love the way you coach! You teach discipline, fundamentals, and all the skills my son needs to not only succeed on the court but in life. I would love for him to play for you!"

I respond with something like, "Thank you so much. It's the way I'm built I guess. I'm glad good coaching is still appreciated."

"Absolutely, I'll tell you what, if you can match the offers we have received I'll put him on your team. He has been offered $5,000/month and all expenses paid for us to attend all the events. Plus, the use of a car for the summer."

I laugh and say, "Expect a call from the NCAA soon."

I estimate that I have had sixty parents say things like this to me over the years! One time, a player and his mother said to me,

"My coach paid me $10,000 to play for him, is that a violation because he said it's not?"

It's a free for all out there! I have many more stories but I hope you get the gist of it.

DOES MY SON NEED THE AAU?

NO! He doesn't!

If your son is good, he will get recruited to a good college. Trust me, I've seen it happen time and time again. He does not need the AAU system and/or the coaches. Many players go to college and then the NBA from the AAU circuit because their parents think it's the only way. It isn't.

He just needs to attend the right camps and play hard. If he's a top level talent, he'll get his name out there. There are ways to do that while avoiding the AAU system completely. This has been done before and should be done more often. That's the saddest and most amusing part of the entire AAU system: It's not necessary.

It's a scam.

CHAPTER 7

NCAA

THE NATIONAL COLLEGIATE ATHLETIC ASSOCIATION – THE NCAA

Have you ever seen the NCAA Rule Book? It's about as thick as a Los Angeles Yellow Pages! I wish I were kidding. Simply put, there are just too many rules and too many regulations. So many that it's nearly impossible to monitor all of them. Because of the improbability of monitoring them all, the rule breakers aren't deterred from committing violations. If someone wants to commit a violation, they will. There is very little the NCAA seems to be able to do about it.

WHY SUCH A BIG BOOK?

There are some rules in society that we take much more seriously than others. For example, not committing a homicide is a rule that most of us don't break; however, coming to a complete stop at a stop sign or jaywalking are rules I think everyone breaks. The ways laws are created stem from someone at one time doing something that someone else complained about. The complaint made logical sense, so a law was created so there would be repercussions if someone else committed the same act. The laws continue to pile up as we age as a nation, and laws that were established 200 years ago have come along for the ride. Even though they no longer make sense, they're still laws.

The NCAA Rule Book is so big because of old rules that are still active and, as people find ways to circumvent fair play, new rules are constantly being added. It really is like the Wild West. People find different ways to cheat or circumvent the system in order to get a competitive advantage. Once the way in which they operated is discovered, a new rule comes out so that the next person can't repeat the same process without consequence.

As a result, we have some ridiculous rules in the rule book. Some of them even contradict other rules! A coach cannot loan a player airfare to fly home for a parent's funeral, even if it's documented that the player paid back the loan. It was even reported that a player could not use his coach's phone to make a phone call! In some cases, a college coach is not allowed to have a player over to his house for dinner or depending on the time of year, he can't speak to his player over the phone at all. The reason for these seemingly idiotic rules is that there have been coaches who have used these innocent manners of communication to illegally recruit players or somehow break a rule.

Idiotic rules are prevalent in society. Thus, they filter into our game, and nowhere is this more evident than in the NCAA, where players make millions of dollars for their respective schools a year but can't profit from it.

Check out some of these idiotic rules/laws we still have in our country today:

- In Maine, it's illegal to have Christmas lights up after January 14.
- In Nevada, it's illegal for a man to buy drinks for more than three people at a time.
- In North Dakota, beer and pretzels cannot be served at the same time in any restaurant.
- In my state of Connecticut, a pickle is not officially a pickle unless it bounces.
- In Michigan, anyone over the age of twelve may own a handgun as long as he/she has not committed a felony.
- If you ever find yourself driving at night through rural parts of Pennsylvania, state law requires that you stop every mile to send up a rocket signal.
- When parking your elephant at a meter in Orlando, FL, be sure to deposit the same amount of change as you would for a regular motor vehicle.
- It's against the law to educate dogs in Hartford, CT.

These laws are not only outdated but were ridiculous when they were first established. However, someone once did something that another person reported and these types of laws came to be. The NCAA rulebook is filled with similar fluff. It is difficult to make sense of all the rules through all of the clutter. There was an incident where the coach paid a player $10,000 for a summer job; his job was turning off the gym lights. Now, players on scholarships can't get side jobs! It's not that the NCAA doesn't want these kids to earn money, it's that they don't trust the coaches, boosters, and scouts who will look for any way to pay a player an inordinate amount of money for menial work and try to disguise a bribe-payment for real employment.

Did you know that the coaching staff of a university can't work their player out during the offseason for more than two hours a week? How is the player supposed to develop his skills, under whose supervision? We get kids not learning the fundamentals in the AAU system who go to college and, for eight months out of the year, they can barely work out with their program. It cripples the development of an already fundamentally weak player!

A certain recent national champion coach has left not one, but two programs on probation for rules violations. Let that sentence sink in for a minute. This coach got caught for a rules violation at a school but was allowed to go to another school. Then, he got caught for violating the rules at that school but, again, he was allowed to go to another school. At the third school he won a national championship and got the acclaim of being a national champion coach. His former students and school paid the price for his infractions with sanctions. Doesn't sound fair does it? Isn't the NCAA supposed to regulate fairness?

Players commit violations all the time. I've heard these excuses: "Well, he never put money in my hand" or "I think he might have helped my dad out, but I wasn't there." That excuse actually passed recently for a player under investigation. The NCAA, in its infinite wisdom, found no wrongdoing by the player and let him participate in the championship game. A year later, I hear that players were exchanging gear for tattoos and they suspended those players for about five games. The inconsistency is ridiculous! It gives the impression that the NCAA is like the Gestapo, and they just randomly go after people they don't like and leave the higher profile player or coach alone.

I have personally reported over twenty-five rule violations to the NCAA. Only rarely, had I seen or heard of punishment being doled out in those circumstances. I'm not saying that the NCAA never investigated my allegations but it's not as if they have subpoena power. When the NCAA finds out a coach has been lying, that's when he really gets in trouble; I've seen coaches fired for lying more often than for committing the violation.

In my personal estimation, I would say that approximately eighty five percent of the programs across the country have someone on their staff right now that has committed or will commit a rules violation. Remember, I run and work at basketball camps across the United States. Division I, II, and III level talents go to these camps. I rub shoulders with the players, their parents, college coaches, scouts, pro players, boosters, superfans, and various levels of athletic departments. I can't say that I see it all, but I would say that I see more than most. Cash payments, benefits, advantages, and academic violations seem to be the most common and, funny enough, the punishment for those things are most severe. It looks as if they aren't too scared of the punishment. Then there are too many phone calls, too many texts, sending gifts, giving out tickets to family members... the list is endless, it really is.

THE FISHING STORY

When a program gets flagged, they can't believe it. The excuse is often: Everyone is doing it! They always say, "Everyone is doing it!" They just love to yell out, "Everyone is doing it!" It reminds me of a story I heard about a cop who saw a bunch of cars speed past his hiding spot. He pulls out, turns on his sirens, and pulls one of the speeders over. The perpetrator gets upset, "Why did I get stopped, they were all speeding too!"

"Have you ever been fishing?" the cop asks.

"Yeah sure, but what does that have to do with this?"

"Have you ever caught all the fish?"

The way the system is now, the NCAA is not equipped to catch every rule breaker, partially because many of the rules are bogus and partially because people are finding loopholes in the old traps.

ONE AND DONE

The better the player, the more programs go after him. The more programs that go after him, the more a program has to do to get him. When everybody is playing by the same rules, every program can only offer the same thing, the differentiators are the coaches themselves, the history, the current roster, and the location. Let's face it, playing at UCLA in Southern California beats playing in Juno, Alaska. However, when you have the titans of Division I recruiting the same player, they all have these differentiators, so the program that finds a way to sweeten the pot usually gets the player. Of course, the pot is a witch's brew of foul-play, but the player doesn't care. He will only be there for one year. If it gets reported, by the time it goes through the process, the season will be over and he'll be playing in the NBA.

The One and Done rule, in my opinion, was created out of haste. However, it's important to note that this is an NBA rule! Currently, the NBA's Collective Bargaining Agreement stipulates that players must have been out of high school for one year and nineteen years old before they can enter the NBA.

There is a great article on mavsblog.dallasnews.com regarding the One and Done rule. It states that the new NBA commissioner Adam Silver is on record saying he would like the requirements to be increased to two years out of high school and 20 years old. Mark Cuban, owner of the Dallas Mavericks, said he would like the minimum requirements to be three years removed from high school and 21 years old.

"Either way," Cuban says, "the current system is too flawed and not in the best interest of 19-year-olds who attempt to jump to the NBA when they aren't ready, maturity-wise.

"Because the NCAA rules are so hypocritical, there's absolutely no reason for a kid to go (to college for one year)," Cuban says. "Because he's not going to class, right? He's actually not able to take advantage of all the fun because the first semester he's there, he starts playing basketball.

So if the goal is just to graduate to the NBA or be an NBA player, go to the D-League. And hopefully at some point we'll have some kind of a secondary draft like baseball, where you can draft a kid starting in the third round and let him play in the D-League."

Cuban emphasized several times that these are his opinions, not that of the NBA's leadership, though Cuban is hardly alone in believing the One and Done rule doesn't work.

"I don't think a lot of (college) coaches like One-and-Done," he said. "I think it helps enable all the bastardized AAU scenarios.

It helps create graft (corruption) with agents. I just think there's absolutely no upside to One-and-Done."

Let me just say that I don't always agree with Mark Cuban, however, sometimes I do!

It appears that just about everyone has an opinion on when a player should be eligible for the NBA. I certainly have mine. My opinion stems from the decline of great basketball on a whole instead of by the player.

THE EXPLOITATION BUSINESS

Schools are making millions and billions of dollars on the backs of their student-athletes. If that is a shock to you, maybe you should find a new rock to live under. So much of the corruption and people profiting from it would go away from the great game of basketball if the NCAA did the right thing: pay them. Now, it's a complicated process I'm sure; however, it's not as complicated as some think.

Life isn't fair. I don't believe that each student athlete should be paid equally. After all, this isn't a socialist country. Certain athletic programs/teams make more money than others, and the kids in teams that make more money for the school should be paid more.

There are quantifiable ways to find out how much each team brings in, such as television contracts, bowl bids, attendance records, merchandise sales, parking, concessions, and more. It can get even more complicated when you add up the conferences and other variables but there are some financial people that are a lot better than me at it and I'm sure they can get to a number. While it probably can't be seen to the exact penny, you can get a ball-park sum. Once you get an idea of how much that sport brings into the universities, give the athletes a small percentage of those profits. I do mean small! I'm not talking about brand new Mercedes money, I'm suggesting they give these nineteen and twenty year olds money to go out to eat, see a movie, or buy a video game. $500-$700 a month... just throwing it out there.

I personally know plenty of student-athletes that can't afford to do anything outside of campus because they have no money, no means of making more money, and no way to take out a loan. We're talking about a real messed up situation. This is why there are so many vultures circling the decay of the NCAA. These kids need money! So they find other means of surviving which inevitably result in rules infractions, cheating, lying, covering up, and a college quality lesson in criminal activity. All the while, the university is rolling in the money from people that watch these kids play!

Here's where I get politically incorrect. I think a basketball or football player should make more money than say, a gymnast. If that doesn't sound right to you, understand that the money that these schools make from football or basketball is what funds gymnastic, lacrosse, and other sports. If you're a gymnast and you don't like it, I think you're extremely selfish. You should thank these other athletes; it's because of them you got your scholarship and/or you get to compete. This is what college is supposed to do, teach life lessons. If a salesperson sells a million dollars of product and another salesperson sells ten thousand dollars of the same product, they take home a different paycheck, right? You get paid more to be a doctor than a nurse.

There are true crooks out there like dirty politicians or Wall Street fat cat deceivers that should be in jail. There are worse travesties in the world than a football or basketball player getting some money to get by and for the amount to be more than a gymnast. By the way, nothing against the sport of gymnastics, gymnasts are amazing athletes. I'm just making a correlation in the amount of money different sports make for a university and how I would disperse it.

I'LL HAVE A SLICE OF RECRUITING VIOLATION BUT HOLD THE ACCOUNTABILITY PLEASE!

I don't get the lack of accountability at the college ranks, particularly when it comes to repeat offenders. The bottom line is that the penalties are not nearly severe enough. It appears that they aren't deterring many people from breaking the rules.

A SOLUTION?

I think this is a very complicated topic and would take so long to dissect, it would equate to another novel, but in an attempt to keep it simple, one way to police the illegal acts is to form a separate governing authority, not affiliated with the NCAA. An FBI type organization that has subpoena power and will investigate these institutions, including the NCAA, on a more authoritative scale.

CHAPTER 8

THE NBA

MOST PROBLEMS OFTEN START AT THE TOP

For every organization or every family, when there is a problem, it typically starts from the top and trickles down. The world of basketball in the United States is no different. There is a major decline of the American born basketball player and many would argue that it starts at the top: The NBA.

I love the game of basketball. There is nothing more I'd rather watch than the absolute best basketball players in the world play against each other. One might think that as athletes get bigger, stronger, and faster, the NBA product could only get better. The problem is that the best have gotten worse, the good have gotten bad, and the marginal have gotten atrocious. Yeah, I said it. There are NBA players today making millions of dollars a year that are a bigger part of the problem than anything else. As you go on reading this chapter, I want to warn you that I might

107

say something about your favorite player that you won't like. You can agree or disagree, but I'm still going to say it. The NBA today has gotten worse over the last twenty years, not better. I know some of you young NBA fans think that Lebron, Kobe, or Durant are probably the best ever and that once their careers are over, you will be proven correct. It's okay to think that. They might be the best you have ever seen, so you have every reason to think that. How about if I prove to you that this is the weakest version of the NBA we have ever had? Would it make you think again or are you too stubborn? A wise man once said: "Only a fool argues against facts." Let's look at some facts:

The talent in the NBA was more congruent in the early '80s. That means winning a championship at that time was a lot harder than it is today. Let me explain to you what happened to our beloved NBA. In 1988, the NBA added two expansion teams: the Miami Heat and the Charlotte Hornets.

During the expansion, existing NBA teams were able to protect their top seven or eight players. The two expansion teams were able to select from the bottom five players of whatever teams they wanted. Then, the two expansion teams got the top picks in the NBA draft which meant that the bad teams that needed those top picks didn't get them, which meant they got worse... much worse. So now, the expansion teams had top picks and bottom level NBA players and the bad teams didn't get better because they couldn't get the top draft picks.

In 1989, two other franchises were added, the Minnesota Timberwolves and the Orlando Magic. The same thing happened again! The good teams stayed good and the average teams got bad and the four expansion teams started off bad. Suddenly, we had people in the NBA that were not good enough for the NBA a year or so prior. Every team got worse. I don't think anyone could argue that point.

Then there was another expansion in 1995 when the NBA added the Memphis Grizzlies and the Toronto Raptors! Not surprisingly, Jordan's Bulls went on their record breaking, seventy-two-game win streak, a record that still exists as I write this in 2014. (Although Raptors fans might fondly remember beating the Bulls that year.)

The NBA product has gotten worse on purpose. Why did the NBA do that? For one reason and one reason only:

They did it for the MONEY.

More teams means more fans at more arenas, more merchandise being bought, more television contracts, and all of that means more money.

So now, we have an NBA that, man for man, isn't as good as it once was, but that's not the part that really bothers me. What really bothers me is this: The NBA simply is not full of highly skilled basketball players and it does not provide good role models for kids. I would agree that the league is full of far greater athletes now than before but it hasn't translated to better basketball players!

Compare a regular season college game against a regular season NBA game and the results will startle you.

The differences you will see are the following:

- Players don't play hard in one game and players will play hard in the other.
- Players travel but don't get called for it in one game but players rarely travel and when they do, they get called for it in the other.
- Teams aren't allowed to play a zone defense in one game and teams can in the other.
- Teams have excessive timeouts in one game and teams have fewer in the other.

It's the player that makes millions of dollars a year that doesn't play his hardest.

It's the "professional" that gets away with breaking the fundamental rules of Dr. Naismith's game with traveling and carrying the ball.

It's the NBA team that can't play a zone defense.

It's the NBA team that has far too many timeouts.

Does that make sense to you? Me neither.

Players today make so much money from us fans that you would think they would make it a personal responsibility to be good role models! You would think that they would continue to work on their craft so they are deserving of your money. The truth is, the players get these huge contracts before playing and earning it. Instead of hard-working role models, we have guys like Dwight Howard. Do you remember the way he manipulated the chaos in Orlando? Then how he went to the Lakers and, because he wasn't the top guy, how that team plummeted? How did he get rewarded? With a huge contract! Stop it NBA, you're embarrassing yourself.

There is a sense of entitlement from NBA players that erodes the ethics and values of the game to the younger generation of players. At the grassroots level, you have sixth graders who will make a three pointer and pound on their temples with three fingers a la their favorite NBA player, instead of running back to play defense. These kids can put the ball between their legs but they can't set a solid screen nor do they want to!

I am a proud American and basketball is an American game. The world is catching up and I don't like it. When I coach, I never advise the youngsters to watch an NBA game over a college game (and the college game is getting just as bad with the One and Done). Soon, some other country will become the dominant basketball country! Kudos to those countries that love the game and teach it the way it should be taught. This is part of the reason they are catching up. The other part is that we are slipping. We are evening the playing field by ourselves.

In the international game, you can't just bulldoze people off the block offensively, you can't travel, and you can't carry the ball. They acquire more skills than jumping high and flashy dribbling. Because they are better at enforcing and teaching the rules, they have better play! The coaches are respected as coaches and as people to learn from. The coaches are in charge, not the players and not the players' union. I wasn't surprised when Brandon Jennings could not get off the bench in Europe. European players are expected to be coachable and team oriented. Sure, he had skills, but not the qualities that enhance a team. Then, Jennings came to the NBA and was an immediate Rookie of the Year candidate. Why? He learned how to play the game the right way, but he didn't learn that here in the U.S.

What do I say about the state of the NBA big man? Sure they can jump and flex, but if Dwight Howard is the epitome of a big man today, how far have we fallen as a country in regards to basketball? The Center position is rarely seen any more in the NBA All-Star game and you know why? The American Center is non-existent.

It's one thing for the skills of the game to erode, but what is unacceptable to me is to have the level of character dissipate. The NBA provides the absolute worst role models in all of sports in my opinion, with NFL wide receivers and corner backs coming in at a close second. Just listen to some of these NBA players speak. Oh wait, you may have never heard them speak. We always get the "NBA Sponsored Spokesman" doing interviews, such as Kobe, Duncan, Lebron, Durant, and CP3. Some of those other guys though, they are an embarrassment to themselves. I don't think you can call their language English! It is a true testament to how they have been coddled and aided throughout their years of school because of their athletic gifts. I've talked to hundreds of them at my camps before they became NBA players and they talk just as bad now as they did then.

How about their behavior? You laugh, but I'm serious. Some of them act inappropriately, they drink and drive, they have domestic violence incidents, they have weapons charges, and the list of illegal and immoral behavior goes on and on. They shoot at people, party all night, they abuse their bodies with alcohol, and the pot smoking is just ridiculous. The league doesn't test for marijuana during the off-season. It does random tests up to four times a year. After the fourth test, gentlemen, light your blunts. The percentage of NBA players that supposedly smoke is staggering.

Then, there is the lack of humility. Why can't you hit a shot and not hoot and holler? Is it a new rule that you have to scream after a dunk or stick your tongue out after a good play?

Kobe Bryant and Lebron James are arguably the two best basketball players in the last ten years. No matter how much the

NBA tries to pass them off as great guys, Kobe might go down as one of the worst teammates in the history of the NBA, in my book. Lebron, to me, is the man that let down his entire hometown city and ran like a coward to form up with other great players to form a "super team" because he could not win on his own being the primary leader. Then, there are the icons and wannabe role models. They wear glasses with no lenses, elementary school backpacks, and have hairstyles designed to attract attention. Can someone tell them that they're already famous and they don't have to do those things for attention? Do you know why they wear the glasses without lenses? It started as an attempt to look like Clark Kent. Do you remember that Clark Kent would wear the "nerd" black rimmed glasses? So now, we have a bunch of athletes wearing glasses they don't need and taking out the lenses to show people that they are in their "Clark Kent mode." I wish someone would tell them that the whole reason Superman wore the glasses was to not attract attention to himself. I think they're missing the point.

All in all, the NBA is about as poor a place for kids to learn anything from as any. You can't learn how to be a better person by watching the NBA. You can't learn about loyalty or how to follow the rules either. The worst part is, you can't even learn how to play basketball correctly from watching the NBA because they don't play it correctly.

Coach Taylor, how would you fix the NBA?

I'm glad you asked! The NBA is the way it is because the players can get away with their actions. It's elementary. There is a way to stop the drinking and smoking problem though: Put in harsher punishment for violators.

NFL teams cut players when they don't perform to the level of their contract. Let's start with some of that! See how long those players will continue to play lazy.

Make it mandatory that all rookies attend a seminar on how to speak correctly. The NBA does have a decent program for rookies but, I think, as some players get settled into their careers, they forget the lesson on public speaking. At the end of the day, these players are representing you, and I'm talking to the NBA here.

Eliminate four teams. It will immediately increase the level of play all across the league. Come on, some of these guys with contracts are jokes!

Play a sixty game schedule. It will make the games matter more, like in college, and extend the careers of most players.

Make all playoff games a best out of five.

These changes will bring back the casual fans and make for a much more exciting NBA.

Suspend players for three years for every DUI conviction and then bring their pay to the league minimum for the next two years or the remainder of their contract. These players make enough money to hire drivers anyway. This would eliminate about ninety-five percent all drinking and driving incidents.

Suspend all players with domestic violence or drug convictions for three years. Again, give them the minimum payment for the next two years.

Too harsh? Really? It's too hard to ask adults that we pay millions of dollars to, to be stand up citizens? In case you didn't know, if you want to drill down to the core of it all, the owners don't pay the players, we do!

How is the NBA responsible for the decline of youth basketball?

Most players just aren't good enough role models. Young, impressionable kids imitate what they see. Is this the behavior you want your child to imitate? We have hundreds of thousands of kids mimicking NBA players even though they aren't in the NBA. So now, society has all of these uneducated, spoiled, entitled, and selfish kids that we have to deal with. These kids become a nuisance to their families and their communities.

The NBA I Want

I want a better NBA. I want an NBA with players, coaches, and owners that display better character. I want them to speak intelligently or, at least, so that I can understand them, foreign players excluded. I want an NBA that plays the game the way it should be played: that doesn't travel, that doesn't carry the ball, and that doesn't flop. I want an NBA that gives to communities and not only improves the sport, but society as a whole.

When an organization has as much money as the NBA does, I think they should do more. Don't you? Have you ever asked yourself what type of NBA you would like? Maybe you should.

CHAPTER 9

COACH TAYLOR'S ADVICE

Ever since I started working at basketball camps, I have been told by people that I bring a different message to the players and parents and that it's refreshing. I have been bombarded over the years with pleas to write a book. Over the last twenty-plus years, I have accumulated great insight into the development of basketball players and how to best work within the system to give someone the best chance of using basketball to further their education or even make it their career. Countless numbers of NBA players have been through my camps with many others playing overseas or coaching at the high school and collegiate level. I have been blessed to sit at the feet of great coaches such as John Wooden and work with the best athletes in the world. I have also witnessed first-hand the mistakes players and parents make and how they never recover from them.

If you're a young player or a parent of a player and want to know the best way to navigate through the murky waters of today's AAU system and the world of personal training, tournaments, camps, skill development, or college recruiting, I believe the following can help. No one is more invested in the happiness and success for your child than you! So you, as a parent, need to be way more involved in the decision making process and stop deferring to these AAU coaches and personal trainers. Here is sort of my "blueprint" for players and parents to follow.

1. <u>Should my child play more games?</u>

> This might sound backwards but some people just don't get it. It's all about PRACTICE, not GAMES. If you have a child between the ages of nine and

fifteen, your child should practice or workout out at least five times for every game they play in. Games are vital mainly to uncover your weaknesses. You will not improve your weaknesses by playing games. You need to build up your weaknesses through practice and gauge your progress through games. If you have to choose between missing a game or a practice, miss the game and go to the practice, or as the parent, miss watching the game and take your child to practice.

2. Does my child need a personal trainer?

Maybe, but it's not that simple. First, ask yourself if you can afford to hire a trainer. If the answer is yes, you need to do some research. If you're looking for a basketball trainer, hire a basketball trainer, not a football coach, track coach, or a dietician to do jumping jacks with. You need to find someone that understands the ins and outs of the game of basketball and can help you improve your child's physical attributes and basketball IQ. I have met far too many so-called personal trainers who literally saw some videos and advertised themselves as such. Beware the scammers! At best, you throw away your money. At worst, your child gets hurt. When I trained basketball players, I would give written tests, check their school grades, and watch film with my players. In my opinion, if you have a great high school or middle school coach, you do not need a personal trainer.

Here's the quick checklist of what to look for in a trainer. It's a dirty business full of con-artists so beware:

Do your due diligence! Find out if and where the trainer has played and who they have coached. Ask for referrals. Your best bet is to find a trainer that has coached at the high school or college level. They have a much better understanding of what a player needs.

Do not hire a trainer through a "company." I have been personally involved in one of these "companies" and all they cared about was the money. Basketball training "companies" are scam artists and I would sprint as far away from them as possible. Usually they hire underqualified, inexperienced coaches and only care about money!

Demand that your trainer do video reviews, attend games, and go over their plan for your child with you, as well as the reasons behind it.

Make sure that the trainer looks the part. If your trainer is 5'2 and weighs 320 lbs., you might be able to find someone better. Find a trainer that lives what he/she teaches.

A good basketball trainer should:

Work your child hard. If they're not sweating, they're not working.

Have a profound knowledge of your sport. If he's just a "get in shape" trainer, you are not maximizing your time or money. A good trainer needs to know your child's sport and help build their basketball IQ as much as their physical attributes.

Teach your child drills that he has not been exposed to and not move on until he has mastered them. Repetition works wonders.

Constantly communicate with you. When I trained, I would give written tests, check grades, and watch film with my player. The trainer should provide you with these results.

Have a solid reputation. If they have been doing it long enough, they should have people that give glowing recommendations of working with them. They should also, through "graduating" talented athletes, have connections to the next level.

Provide good feedback. Your trainer should quickly understand your child's strengths and weaknesses and should constantly evaluate his development.

Be brutally honest. It may not be what your child wants to hear but it is what he needs to hear. It should be said respectfully though, not in a demeaning manner.

Not increase your fee without increasing time with your child. Most of the trainers I know are pulling a scam. Some trainers ask for more money if you have a lot of questions, as if they are the only ones with the knowledge or as if you aren't already paying them to make your child better.

Be involved in skill development camps. After all, that's what they profess they are going to do for your child right?

See your child two to four times a week for best results. If you only see the trainer once a week, that's fine as long as the trainer provides you with a weekly game plan. Your child should do skills and drills throughout the week so that the trainer can see improvements. Make no mistake about it, finding the right trainer can be as valuable as anything else regarding your child's development. Just make sure you are getting your money's worth.

3.   <u>Should I send my child to a basketball camp?</u>

I would send my child to skill development camps over the summer, not exposure camps. (Again, this is more directed towards nine to fifteen year olds.) Evaluation camps, camps where the player gets ranked and they only play games, are adequate for the high school rising junior and senior.

You might have to travel a little for the right camp, but it's worth it. Do your research. Look for reviews. Talk to high school coaches or shoot an email to a local college coach. Ask them if they know of any good, high quality skill development camps.

I cannot stress this enough; it is so much more valuable for a players development to attend a hardcore developmental basketball camp over some evaluation camp where all they do is play games. Who cares how good you are in the eighth grade? It's being good in the eleventh and twelfth grade that can positively impact your future. There are thousands of athletic scholarships given every single year. That needs to be your goal!

One of the sad aspects of the game is that a lot of camps have begun focusing more on tournament play than skills development. This is not a good thing! Stop the madness. It comes from the degradation of our coaching society coupled with the laziness of the camp directors. It is much easier to run and direct a tournament than a traditional camp. Running camps is hard work, running tournaments is cake by comparison. Go to a camp that focuses more on drills instead of games.

4. <u>Do games improve my child's play?</u>

I know I'm repeating myself here but that's because it's important. If all you do is play games, you will slowly improve (if at all), but if you focus on drills and skills, your improvement will be quicker. AAU scheduled games won't teach you much and won't help you improve. I learned more from pick-up games at the park against grown men than I ever did playing or a rec. league or AAU team. In most cases, AAU games are a glorified recess.

I equate games to a math test. If a student fails a math test, does the teacher give him four more tests or does the teacher provide lessons? The teacher will give you homework, re-teach the sections you had problems with, and then maybe re-test you at the end of the week.

5. How do I choose which AAU team to play for?

Do some research! Begin the process by not trusting everything you hear from a coach. You have to understand that most AAU coaches only care about themselves and their records. A coach might love your kid if he's really good but won't help develop your kid. At the end of the day, your kid will give that coach a better resume so he can parlay it into a better coaching job and your kid will not improve personally or as a player.

126

Check the coach's references and fact-check his resume. Observe the practices. Observe the games. Speak to other coaches. Don't be afraid to pull your kid out of a team if the coach doesn't behave or speak to the kids the right way.

You need to understand the level of influence an AAU coach will have over your child. Some kids respect their coaches more than their parents, so make sure that his coach is saying the right things and behaving the right way!

In a perfect world, your high school team plays together during the summer, even if the head coach can't be there. As a high school coach, I would never want my players playing for someone I did not know or approve of. I took it as an insult when I would prepare my team to stay together with a plan over the summer and a parent would inform me that their child was going to play elsewhere for someone who I had never even heard of. The bottom line is, if your high school has a good plan for the off-season, you do not need to play AAU basketball. Just go to the right skill development camps and play with your high school team.

6. <u>My son's school isn't known as a basketball school, should I transfer him to another school?</u>

Personally, I would never transfer my child to a "better basketball school." The only reason I would transfer my child is for academic, social, or safety reasons. It's better for your child to play on a team that barely qualified for the playoffs but he is the man on than to play sparingly with limited minutes at a "basketball factory" school where he can't display his full array of talents.

Too many parents transfer their kids out of schools because of a few losses. It's ridiculous. The scouts understand when a great young player is playing with lesser talent and will not judge the player because of the team's record.

Don't do the Lebron thing and abandon ship to a "better team" for a shot at the division or state title. Tell your child to stay where his friends are, make them better, and expand their game. Teach them how to be a leader! Don't transfer to play with better players, don't be a coward. Man up. I work with kids all across the country and they see what Lebron did as a sort of cop-out. Teach your child integrity and to have value in his word.

7. Should I keep my kid back a year?

That's been the popular thing for years now. A twelve year old kid has talent and shows potential. The next thing you know the parents are "home-schooling" him or keeping him back a year so that he can play against younger kids. They think it will help their child get a competitive advantage but what they really taught him was they didn't have confidence that he could play well against kids his own age. It shows him how to cheat and manipulate the system. What kid actually wants to do another full year of school? Do you realize what you're putting him through? It's bad karma. Don't do it.

8. How do I get discovered?

This is what youth basketball is all about. Most of the other questions are about improving so that you get discovered by colleges that can offer you a scholarship. But once you've followed all the steps

I've laid out and you're a monster on the court, how do you get discovered?

The best way to get discovered is to play in the right basketball camps! Coaches want to see that you have the required skills and athleticism to play for them. The best way to show them your individual skills and athleticism is to attend the right camps, ones that will showcase your talents outside of a game situation. They feel that if they see what they are working with, they can put you in the perfect situation to maximize your effectiveness in a game.

THE RECRUITING PROCESS

Many players and coaches have asked me how to get their child recruited. What's the smart way of going about it? Being a former Division I coach and a current evaluation camp and tournament director, I have some opinions on this matter. I have been successful in guiding hundreds of kids to hundreds of schools on scholastic scholarships. Get out your highlighter and pay attention. It requires work and effort but it more than pays off! What I would do is the following:

1). Have your child make a list of the top ten to twenty universities they would like to attend. Make sure these universities are realistic based on their talent, academic standing, and potential. The schools should be at a level that is appropriate to their talent. They should factor in location, education, and level of play.

2). Once the list is complete, I would call the basketball offices of those universities. I would ask the assistant or head coach where they will be during the spring and summer recruiting months. What tournaments are they attending? What camps? Where? For how long? I would then cross reference all the universities to see which tournaments or camps overlap and then plan on attending those events.

3). I would then research those tournaments and camps to see how well run they are. If it's a camp, how well is the camp operated, who is the camp director, etc. If it's a tournament, research how many teams have attended in the past and how well it has been run. Do the research and due diligence.

4). I would then send DVD's of two or three full, complete, and unedited games to each coach! I never valued a highlight reel and neither do any of the coaches I know, and I know quite a lot of coaches. Hopefully your coach films each game and if not, then your parents, relatives, or friends should video each game you play. This is of extreme importance! You must film as many games as possible and, again, don't edit the video. If you can, set up a website or make a YouTube channel where you can post your videos and have multiple coaches watch the games. This is the trend as of late. If you can afford the cost of developing a website or recording games, I would highly suggest doing this. Then you simply provide the schools you want to attend with a link or a website where they can watch the games on their phones or iPads.

5). Include a bio sheet with each DVD you send or on your website or YouTube channel! Provide as much detail as possible and do not make it a form or template letter (the same to all colleges). Make it personal. Include why you have an interest in their university and program. Include academic and athletic statistics and be accurate. Provide accurate size, weight, wing span, vertical leap, etc. I would obviously include all forms of contact, a photo, and a copy of transcripts if possible!

6). Take the SAT or ACT as early and as often as possible. Include these results in your letter and if you have not taken those tests, send a follow up letter once you receive those scores so the coaches are updated.

7). COMPLETE THE CLEARINGHOUSE PROCESS AS EARLY AS POSSIBLE! Go to NCAA.org for more information on the clearinghouse.

8). Follow up with all of the programs you mailed game film to or provided links to. I would follow up two to three weeks after I sent the DVD. I would follow up with a phone call and/or email.

9). Look into attending the university basketball camps so you can form a relationship with each coach and they can see you live. Do everything you can to get information and be seen by the coaches at the programs you wish to attend. This might not be possible for many people based on the proximity of the universities but this could be very productive if possible.

This is just the beginning. Parents and players must market themselves. How bad do you want it? You have to work! You have to go get it!

WHAT CAN I DO AS A PARENT?

The most important thing, although it should be obvious, is to be supportive. You have no idea how many parents don't know how to be supportive. I have seen parents constantly criticize their child and never praise them. Oh sure, they'll brag about their child until they're blue in the face to anyone that will listen but they won't give their own child the compliment. Do you want to know why? Because their child is a big enough bragger on his own. Do you want to know why? Because the parent never compliments the child so he feels he needs to say it himself. It's a sad little cycle.

Do not put undue pressure on your child. Stop telling your kid how important this game is or how he can't afford to have a bad day today or any of that negative, pressure-building junk. Tell him to play hard and have fun out there. If your child has done all the prep work, the games should be fun.

Be his parent, not his agent. Parents can ruin the experience for the child by trying to double as a sports agent. Come on, you don't know the first thing about being a sports agent so just be a great parent. Teach them right from wrong. Provide rules and direction and, if the situation demands it, follow through on the consequences.

I'll try to say this as nicely as possible: SHUT UP when sitting in the bleachers! I'm not saying don't cheer. Heck, it's your kid out there and if you cheer louder than everyone else, good for you. I'm talking about the idiot parents that are nonstop backseat coaches and front seat complainers. I see a kid getting trapped or double-teamed and hear their parent yell, "Shoot it!" Coaches evaluate the player, but they also evaluate the parents. If a coach or scout hears a parent rooting solely for his child's stats or argue against every call made against his or her child, he might not want to bring that family to his school. College basketball is more about teamwork and making the right basketball play in order to get someone a high percentage shot because everyone on the court can score. If a parent is yelling for their kid to jack up shots, they understand that the kid has been raised like that his whole life and they might not want that mentality ruining their cohesive locker room. You need to be aware of this truth: A parent's behavior in the stands can play a huge role in a coach determining if they extend a scholarship to the player.

Also, continue to stress to your child the importance of grades! The higher the GPA or SAT scores, the more schools that will be open to recruiting your child. Parents do not understand the massive importance a student's grades are for the recruiting process. In fact, it's the secret ingredient. If a player has a 4.0 GPA and a 2200 SAT score, there will be one hundred schools that will actively recruit the player. That means that your child will be seen by many more schools. At least they will be seen and if a player isn't seen, he isn't recruited. Conversely, a player with a 2.0 GPA and a 900 SAT score might be seen by a few schools. Kids that graduate high school with these sorts of academics will, most likely, have to attend a prep school or a junior college, which adds an extra year or two where anything can happen.

Unfortunately, I have seen many talented ball players go down this tunnel and never emerge on the other side. If they aren't disciplined enough to get good grades in high school, they most likely aren't disciplined enough to attend a junior college where they have a lot more freedom and come out with better grades. A kid that can play and has great grades will be able to pick and choose which school to go to. That caliber of person will also be able to pick and choose where they go in life but it must be taught early. You need to instill these character traits in them. A player with poor grades gets discussed by the coaches as lazy or not very smart; neither one is a good thing!

When I was a college coach, I would receive a huge database of players with their grades. If I saw a GPA of 3.5 or higher, I had the secretary send them a form letter looking for more information to gauge their interest. If the player replied, I would do my best to watch him play at some point in the summer, either in person or by video. I completely ignored players if they had a GPA around 2.0.

When I would go to camps and see a player I liked, the first thing I would do is find out their GPA. If it was too low, I wouldn't touch him.

Studying and getting good grades are not only vital to getting into a good school, but will help you when your basketball days are over. You have to have a Plan B. Your basketball career is only an injury away from being over. Then what?

PHYSICAL / MENTAL / EMOTIONAL PREPARATION

We are talking about athletes here so let's start with their physical health. Stay away from drugs and alcohol. Drugs and alcohol are major causes of setbacks in life regardless of the profession. For athletes, they're killer. Not only do they start to affect your psyche, competitive drive, and memory, among other things, they also ruin your reputation. Remember, you are who you hang out with!

Parents, be aware of who your kid is hanging out with. If they run with a bad crowd, you likely have a bad kid. If he runs with bad students, you likely have a bad student. If he runs with the pot smoking crew, you likely have a pot smoking kid. Coaches inevitably find out the circle your kid hangs out with; be aware of that. Steer your child the right way.

Eat well. Teenagers can eat anything and they do, but if you want to leverage your athletic ability to get a free ride to a major university, you need to know how much competition you have. If you eat better than the other guy, advantage you!

Sleep well. There are countless studies that show sleeping helps you athletically. In one particular instance, five swimmers were monitored as part of a study in 2008. These swimmers extended their sleep to ten hours a day for seven weeks. At the end of the study, the athletes could swim faster and react more quickly. Sleep also helps your growth, improves your immune system, helps you concentrate better, and makes you look better. Early to bed, early to rise, nothing good happens after midnight anyway.

Preparing yourself mentally doesn't mean getting amped up in the locker room and running out of the tunnel yelling like a mad man. Preparing yourself mentally means taking the time to be a student of the game. You need to know the nuances of the game and game situations like when to make a pass, when to shoot, when to go for the shot block and when to step in and take a charge. You need to know where you are most effective on the floor. There are kids that can score from all over but there is always a spot on the floor where their field goal percentage is higher. You need to find that spot. The smarter the player on the court, the better the player.

You also need to study the game, not watch it as a fan. This makes a huge difference. When you watch a televised game, remember that most of the color commentators were former players or coaches and you can learn a lot from their insight. You have no excuse not to be a smart basketball player. The knowledge is everywhere; you just have to want to capture it. Even if your coach isn't a great X's and O's guy, you have guys like Van Gundy, Hubie Brown, Jay Bilas, and other great basketball minds sharing their knowledge to those who want to obtain it. Your competition wants to obtain it; you need to want to as well.

NO GIRLFRIENDS – Girlfriends at the high school level for a player with high level talent is a killer to that player's chances of playing at the next level. Stop thinking of the here and now and think about your future. Girls mess with your head. I have been doing this for a long time and I have known of thousands of kids that had promising careers until they started dating or "fell in love." What is going to happen when you get accepted to a school far away? Where will your mind be? How about when scouts come to see you play and your "girlfriend" is in the stands next to a guy you don't like or your girlfriend isn't even there? The more time you give your girlfriend, the less time you have to develop your skills or sleep well.

MENTAL TOUGHNESS

This is what separates the good from the great, the bad from the good. Mental toughness is a huge intangible. If a player is mentally tough, they have the best chance to succeed. They will be able to adapt and overcome. I know of a player named Luke who played football. Luke felt that he was not being treated well and was basically ignored. However, he didn't quit and he didn't whine. Instead, that boy went to work. He was mentally tough! He got stronger, faster, quicker, and better. He "forced" the coaches to play him. He went on to receive all state honors, walked on to a BIG TEN football team, made the team, and is playing on the team currently. That is a mentally tough kid! Mental toughness is a great character trait to have!

Mental toughness is the ability to accept criticism, the ability to fall down and get back up on your own, the ability to fail and overcome that failure, the ability to succeed against the odds, the ability to achieve greatness despite your limitations, and the ability to maximize your potential! Mental toughness, in my opinion, is the most important thing an individual athlete can have. It's even more important than talent!

WHAT DO COACHES LOOK FOR IN A PLAYER?

Every coach has their own particular style of offense and defense that they like to deploy, so they look for players that will fit into their scheme. In that sense, coaches look for specifics unique to their program. However, there are some universal traits that coaches look for and if you don't have them, he won't be looking at you.

This is what coaches look for:

1. A player that can create his own offense. You need to know how to get separation from the defender and play through the contact without forcing your shots.
2. A fundamentally sound player. You need to know the game. Work on your ball handling, passing, and layups

– right handed and left handed layups! You need to do the jump stop correctly without traveling. You need to know how to use your pivot foot. You need to learn what to do from the triple threat position. You need proper shooting form. You need to have a sound defensive stance and know how to slide. You need to have proper footwork. All of these are absolutely essential to play college basketball anywhere.

3. Someone who plays hard. Back in my day, (I know, I hated hearing my coach say that, but it's true), going hard was a given. Nowadays, it's a skill that scouts check off on an evaluation form. It's an acquired skill and you need to acquire it! Coaches love extra-effort players.

4. Players that are coachable. You need to look at your coach in the eye and take whatever criticism he gives you in a positive way. You need to let the coach know that you appreciate his feedback because you know he wants to make you a better player. If the coach thinks you're feeling personally attacked when he is trying to help you improve, he is not going to want to coach you.

5. Resilient players. Don't back down! If someone dunks on you, take the ball back out and go back at him! Don't look at him like a fan and be scared to touch the ball. Don't play scared, don't play weak. We want players that are confident, aggressive, and who are constantly attacking.

6. Players that are mentally strong. Mental toughness is the key to greatness. It's what separates the good from the great and the great from the superstar. Nothing should break your spirit. Nothing should break your will. No one should be able to make you play less than how you can play. If you're losing by twenty, you need to play as hard as you were when it was an even ball game.

7. Players with high basketball IQs. We want to teach our own brand of basketball. We don't want to teach basketball. You should come in already knowing and understanding the game. Know the term KYP – Know Your Personnel. Know the time and scoring situations, when you can take two shots to the other team's one. You need to be able to run multiple offenses and switch on the fly to different defensive sets.

8. Defensively gifted players. This has to do with wanting it. Everybody will play to their best ability when they have the ball and all eyes are on them, but how about when they're on defense? You need to run hard through screens and picks, help your teammate out, close out quickly, contest every shot, block out, and go after loose balls, even if it's going to cost you some floor burns. Defense isn't about talent and athletic ability; it's about IQ and desire. Larry Bird certainly wasn't a naturally gifted athlete compared to other players of his time, but he was a

great team defender and rebounder because he wanted to win and knew how to win. Desire and Intelligence = great defense.

Most coaches agree that not all players can have all these characteristics but it's great to find those that do. Most of these characteristics are easy to obtain because there is a direct correlation with those traits to effort and character. If you don't have a good coach that teaches and preaches this, these traits might not be in your repertoire and you have a serious choice to make.

SACRIFICE

Every player needs to know the true definition of this word! Being great requires sacrifice. Beating out thousands of talented ball players to be recruited by a major program requires sacrifice. These are the things that typically need to be sacrificed for you to get a scholarship that could change your destiny:

1. Partying – You have to stay away from that party scene. Too much drugs/alcohol, too much drama, and too many haters are too many risks for a player with too much talent.

2. Hours at the mall on weekends – Your time will be better served if you work on your skills, son.

3. Sleeping in on weekends – Yes, sleep is good. Go to bed early and get up early so you can go to those camps I mentioned or get to practice.

4. Dating – Girls/Boys will distract you and keep you off track. It takes too much time when you can be studying or honing your skills.

5. Give up your shot – Know when someone has a better look or defer to a better player. You need to know yourself and your role and fill your role as best as you can.

6. Play through pain – Get up and play. I'm not saying to play through an injury. Injuries are serious and require time to heal. However, daily aches and pains are part of the game: Charlie-horses, elbows, floor burns, and burning lungs are all part of the game.

LEARN TO SAY NO!

One of the greatest things a young player can do is say no. Imagine where the conversation would be regarding Len Bias if he had simply said no. He was one of the best players I ever saw in college! You, as a young player, have to say no. Stay away from the party scene, avoid "friends" that do illegal things or participate in illegal activities. Stay away! You can't choose your family, but you can choose your friends and who you hang out with. If you are at a party that gets busted by cops and you get arrested, even if you did nothing wrong and did not participate in any illegal activity, it will be a huge red flag for any college coach that might be recruiting you. You can lose your entire future simply by making that one bad decision.

DETERMINATION

With all the sites available on the web, you can search for drills and do them yourself if need be. Everyone might not be equal with regards to size, but determination is the great equalizer. If you want something, go get it! If you are relentless, you will achieve success. If you have no money, you can succeed if you work hard and want it. If you do not have the resources at home (computer, internet, televisions, DVR's, etc.), then go to a public library, go to a school, or go to a friend's house. There is always a way. You can go on YouTube and find drills to make you better. You can go to thousands of different websites to find recipes for success in basketball or any sport. There are no excuses! GET IT DONE!

You control your destiny, not anyone else. No coach or parent can force you to be great. You have to make the choices, you have to study, you have to say no, and you have to work. This book is intended to leverage the playing field and give you the best chance to fulfill your basketball dream. I am letting you know what you need to do. You need to reach down and find that determination to follow the instructions I've laid out.

Talent without desire becomes wasted potential. Talent coupled with determination can go a long way.

In this chapter I answered a lot of the questions I get answered. Now I have a question for you:

How bad do you want it?

Chapter 10

A SUMMARY OF THE PROBLEM

The AAU System is responsible for the decline of American Basketball.

The AAU has too much power! Almost every talented player believes they need to play AAU ball somewhere in order to be seen by college coaches. It has become a system where predator-type coaches look for sixth and seventh grade high level talent and sink their talons into them in order to make a profit. AAU programs are concerned with making money, not about benefiting kids' lives. A majority of the high level AAU programs are not about to lose money to better kids' lives. They should be great mentors, provide life lessons, and not demand so much money from kids. They should be more concerned about making a difference in kids' lives!

Big shoe companies compensate these AAU coaches (although much less as of late) with money and thousands of dollars of merchandise to give these players and their parents.

They want to make sure that they don't miss out on any future stars wearing their gear. This exploitation has brought back the dirty side to the pure sport of basketball.

Chris Paul, of the Los Angeles Clippers, credits his experience in AAU as to why he's the player he is today and I'm sure there are many other NBA players that feel the same. The problem is that for every one person that made it to become a professional basketball player, there are thousands that didn't who could have. In general, AAU usually makes a player worse.

The casual fan doesn't quite understand because it's "amateur basketball" but this is big business. If an AAU coach finds the right talent, he could earn over six figures by enabling his players to wear a particular brand. It is a raw form of propaganda. It has created a legion of so-called coaches who try to be more like agents. The system is now a breeding ground for unscrupulous people teaching unethical lessons to young teenage kids. In order for him to convince players to play for him, he promises them the world. He tells them that they are bound for the NBA and provides them with the coolest gear a player could want. The kids and their parents start to believe them. They start to live a life of entitlement and lose focus on vital areas of their lives that they need to develop. Academics and fundamental behaviors receive the most collateral damage. Knowledge based coaches have been replaced by slick talking salesmen who understand the art of recruiting better than the sport of basketball.

Because the actual imparting of basketball knowledge is a weakness for most of the AAU coaches, they put together more tournaments and far less coaching camps. The player with talent believes that he needs to be on one of the traveling teams in order to be seen and for his fame to grow. Have you ever seen a game where every player is trying to be the star? It's the ugliest form of basketball and, sadly, it's called the highest level of amateur basketball. So today, when the rest of the world is practicing their fundamentals and learning the nuances of the game, we have hall of fame players complaining about practice and uncouth coaches getting their teams into tournaments instead of camps because they can't run a camp and can't profit from sending their kids to one. This is the cycle we have been perpetuating for years now. This cycle is now the norm and I see the beginning of the end in terms of the United States being the premier power in basketball.

Listen to me; we need to get back to the camp format. Fewer tournaments, more camps. If I were the Supreme Commander of amateur basketball, I would disassemble most of the tournament play and run basketball camps everywhere. Camps improve a player's skill far more than a tournament. So why are players signing up to play tournaments?

People often ask me: Coach Taylor, how would you improve the game of basketball? Where would you start? My answer: I would have a lot more camps and a lot fewer tournaments. Indulge me for a moment and go through this scenario with me.

If we were to select teams of thirteen year olds and you took the top five best and most athletic kids and left me with the bottom half, your team would beat mine. Now, in three years, if your five go the AAU route and I take my five to developmental camps, my team would beat your team of better athletes. In two more years, they would be seniors in high school and their basketball futures could be on the line, and my team would crush your team by forty points. Now, imagine if I had the top five kids to begin with?

So Coach, you don't think my son needs to play games? That's not what I'm saying. Your son should be playing as many pickup games as he can. He will hone his game on the blacktop. He should also play games in the camps that you send him to. The key is in choosing the right event.

The problem is that there are not NCAA certified camps in every major city. I would establish NCAA certified camps in NY, LA, Chicago, Dallas, Miami, Denver, Boston, Cleveland, and in every major city in between. I would make it financially feasible for more kids to be able to attend. We would have great developmental camps with games in between and no tournaments. This would eventually strangle the AAU system to death.

The AAU coach is taking center stage as the high school coach becomes less relevant and it really upsets me! If I couldn't do away with tournaments all together, I would allow only high school coaches that are certified as educators to coach AAU teams in tournaments. That way, high school teams and their coaches could stay together during the off-season and continue to develop. If a player wanted to transfer to another team to somehow improve his "recruiting status," he would have to sit out a year. This musical chair farce we have needs to stop. I would change the ridiculous rule that stipulates a high school coach can't mentor or coach his players in the off-season. This is not the case in every state but it is in many. It just doesn't make sense to me. You have a qualified guy that knows the game and then you don't allow him to continue to develop his players and leave the kids to fend the wolves off by themselves. In the words of Dickie V, "Are You Serious?!"

The high school problem starts with allowing transfers. Coaches are intimidated by the player, fearing that the player will transfer if he gets upset. A scared coach cannot be an effective coach. We need to give high school coaches their mojo back. Enforce the transfer rule the same way they do in college: If you transfer, you need to sit out a year. Of course, if it's a legitimate move, you should be allowed to play. As of right now, there are no rules for transferring players and, at the end of the day, it's the player that gets hurt by it. Without guidelines, kids falter. A world without discipline is a world of anarchy. Too many talented kids do not have discipline because they have been coddled by the AAU system and the high school rules which allow them to transfer at a whim.

I would take things a step further and fine the parents $10,000.00 if they are found guilty of these violations. I would. I would also fine them every time they or their kid trumped up a false charge against a coach. Uncouth parents and their undisciplined children have ruined the lives of too many good coaches. People that tried to teach the game with values and ethics have been run off. The ramifications of not having that coach there has been detrimental to all the other kids who had a much weaker coach because the good coach had to leave or was let go. You better believe I would protect those coaches and fine those families.

The bottom line is this: We have a lot of work to do, assuming of course you would want a better system. It starts with eliminating AAU basketball.

Chapter 11

THE SOLUTION PART 1

I have identified the problem. The problem is the AAU and a lot of AAU coaches and some players are upset. Understand AAU coach, I don't want to eliminate your job and not give you an alternative. Yes, I do want to get rid of the vultures and if that's you, then I take it back. I do want to eliminate your job. You suck at it anyway. To the other AAU coaches (especially those that also coach at a high school or middle school), I would like to have you involved in certified camps and proactively teaching kids the game of basketball. Sure, some of you may not get huge salaries anymore but if you were in it solely for the money, then you're in the vulture pile. To the player that is upset I say this, I'm only trying to make you better. Slow down and hear me out. Now, if you're a lazy, entitled player that thinks the world owes you something because you can dunk the ball, you may have to actually work on your game because a lot of other kids are going to be getting a heck of a lot better if they follow my advice.

The truth is that I'm not the first person to rail against AAU basketball. In fact, I believe it was 2008 when everyone agreed that AAU basketball was a problem, so they set out to fix it. Oh yeah, the NBA and NCAA got together and formed an initiative to fix the problem. At the time, I thought nothing could be better for the sport! I was so happy to hear that all the key organizations were going to work together to make basketball better. What a great idea!

I remember that they had five areas of concentration.

1. Building strong communities. We were to have one uniform website/social media outlet. There had never been one site where kids, coaches, and parents could turn to in order to get good information on how to improve

a players skill, talents, learning, coaching tips, parental responsibilities, and so on.

2. Educating Athletes. Provide more national summer camps and skills programs to better the players, particularly at national events.

3. Supporting Coaches. Create a universal coaching education program that would emphasize what it is to be a coach, teach a coaches code of conduct, a certification process, and educational programs.

4. Developing officials. Concentrate on youth basketball officials to assist them in interpreting the rules properly at a national level.

5. Sanctioned events for youth competition. They would work with existing credible organizations that ran events to establish a national standard for all future events. They would also have a national calendar that would work with the prerequisites such as the clearinghouse and other hurdles that allow a player to be eligible to play in the NCAA.

This was the plan. I loved it. Unfortunately, it just didn't pan out as everyone expected, certainly not as well as I expected it to. The website wasn't a total flop. The website called ihoops started off strong but wasn't properly promoted. To prove my point, some of you may be hearing of ihoops for the first time.

This is the NBA, the NCAA, and youth basketball organizations from across the country getting together. You would expect for every player or at least every coach to know about it right? Also, the site in and of itself isn't very user friendly.

The second, third, fourth, and fifth areas of concentration (educating athletes, supporting coaches, developing officials, and sanctioned events) have been total flops. I have no knowledge of any programs on educating athletes or sanctioned events. If there is a new program that supports coaches and develops officials on a national level, I haven't heard of it either and I work with high-level youth talent for a living! Simply put, the initiative failed. My colleagues and I put on the events/camps that this alliance was supposed to do.

It was a great idea, but it wasn't backed with a concerted effort. It reminds me of those kids with a ton of athletic and natural talent that don't back up their game with hard work and determination. Those players never become as good as people expect them to be. The reason why there was never a real concerted effort, in my opinion, is that at the end of the day, it didn't make anyone any money. This initiative had a feel-good story all over it but there was no financial gain for players, the NBA, the NCAA, NCAA coaches, or shoe companies. There was no immediate or long-term financial gain, so we got pretty lip-service backed by half-ass attempts.

So, now what? All of the governing bodies of basketball in America, including the NBA, got together and they failed. What can be done to fix the game in this country?

The sport of basketball has fallen far since the '80s and '90s. In the '80s, Bird and Magic captivated people from Boston and Los Angeles and everywhere in between. Then came Michael Jordan with his disciplined determination and gravity-defying ability. Stockton to Malone was the quintessential clinic on how to run the pick and roll and the Round Mound of Rebound proved that at 6'5, you could lead the league in rebounding if you wanted it bad enough. Then came the Dream Team! That was it, the pinnacle, the summit. The decline started so slowly that no one noticed it for years. The NBA has lost countless fans since then and for good reason. The players we once looked up to are retired. The best player in the world gave up on his city and colluded with other stars from other teams to win not one, not two, not three...

Now we are seeing nicknames on jerseys? For you fans that think it's about fun, don't be so naïve. It's about making more money. Millions of people already have a Lebron James jersey but they don't have a King James jersey. Then, there were conversations about adding a 4-point play? Really? How about when they talked about lengthening and widening the court? That was just stupid. Don't even get me started about the All-Star game. I'm not alone, the greatest basketball man alive today, Mr. Jerry

West, said the game is the worst it has ever been. As usual, Mr. West is right!

Hey NBA, superficial changes won't bring back the fans that left and it won't bring you new fans either. I know you want to make more money, but let me tell you a secret: If you want to get more fans to make more money, you need to change the game back to how it's supposed to be played.

What do you think Coach Taylor? How would you fix the game?

My answer to this might sound ridiculous to some of you, maybe all of you, but you need to know that I'm going to tell you what is needed to change the game. I'm not looking at dollars and I'm not tiptoeing to make sure I don't hurt people's feelings.

To fix the game of basketball, you need to start at the top, so let's start with the NBA. The game is boring, the players are bad role models, and the skill level has declined. It doesn't make much sense but we have better athletes now playing a worse brand of basketball.

The NBA should:

Subtract the league by two to four teams. The league made a mistake when they expanded in terms of the level of basketball. Imagine if the best players of a few teams go to other teams that needed them. More than that though, the level of play will increase by taking out twenty four to forty eight of the worst players.

Go down to a sixty game schedule. It's just too long of a season. I'm a basketball junkie and my co-writer Eli is too. He gets the league pass every year; we love basketball. The problem is that when the season is so long, there is no urgency for the players or the fans. Right now, the NBA plays an eighty two game regular season. By the time the last couple of weeks roll around, the first six or seven teams are usually set from each division and there are, at most, three other teams jockeying for a playoff spot. That means all these other teams and their fans have lost interest in their teams weeks or maybe even months ago. Imagine if the NBA only played sixty games. Each and every game would count.

The coaches would coach with more urgency, the players would play with more intensity, and the fans would be more fanatical. That sounds like more fun to me. More seats would be filled at some of the half-empty arenas because more teams would have a legitimate shot at making the playoffs.

Better Referees. You might think we have the best referees right now, and we do. They just don't enforce the rules. For goodness' sake red, call the traveling! It almost seems as if the refs are in cahoots with Sports Center and allow an extra step or two if it's followed by an outstanding display of athleticism. If a player carries the ball, call it. If a player is set and the offensive player collides with him, call the charge. If the defensive man beats the offensive player to a spot, call the player control foul. You have people like me who make a living teaching the right way to play basketball but, at the highest level, they are calling it differently. In the words of Marc Jackson, "Come on NBA, you're better than that!"

Rules Changes. Stop coddling. These are some rules that needed to be changed:

> No Advancement on Timeouts in the Last Two Minutes. Why do we magically move the ball? If a team is getting beat, they're getting beat. Why

does the league go against the team that, up to that point, has played better? It's bad enough that you let the ball handlers travel and carry the ball, now you're bringing the ball up for them too? In my only Facebook reference...smh.

A Technical Foul Should Also Be a Personal Foul. I don't think I need to explain the reason for that, do I? It just makes sense. If someone is going to go on a swearing tirade where kids of all ages are present, make it count as one of their six personal fouls per game. Six is too many anyway.

Allow Zone Defenses. We have the best players in the world but we're afraid to let them use whatever defense they want. Is it because we won't get as many highlight dunks? Is it because the league is made of athletes and not shooters and the scoring would come down? Come on; let us see Coach Popovich use his full arsenal of basketball knowledge against Coach Thibodeau. If they want to use a zone, let them! Don't hinder their usage of personnel.

No Timeouts Except on Dead Balls. They're pros for goodness' sake. They have all the practice time they could want. The NBA should presume that these professional coaches and players will know what to call on-the-fly.

There Should be Fewer Timeouts. Oh wait, then we won't see as many car or beer commercials. We can't do that can we? The game is a tad too long as it is.

There Should Be a Hard Salary Cap. PERIOD.

One and One Free Throws (Like in College). It will bring more excitement to the games. It will also force some of these guys to really practice their free throws.

The Clock Should Not Stop on Made Baskets in the Last Two Minutes. Why should it?

Make a Deeper Three-Point Line. The league is three-point happy. Make them earn it. We have everybody and their mother jacking up threes today. These guys have been playing basketball their entire lives, you can move the line back an extra foot or so.

Come Down Harder on Criminals. Players who
are convicted of felonies should be suspended
for three years if convicted. In most other profes-
sions, you're fired and, most likely, never allowed
to come back. If someone makes it to the NBA and
makes the amount of money they make through
the generosity of the fans, if they can't behave,
find someone who can. Every NBA player is a role
model. I have been places where less than average
NBA players have attended and people still rush
to take pictures with them and get their auto-
graphs. They are looked up to. They should be
suspended and when they come back, it should
be at the minimum salary level. Hey, they would
still make more money than ninety nine percent
of the American workers. The sad thing is, if the
NBA tried to enforce it (not that they would), the
Player's Union would fight it. What would they
say? "Hey, an NBA player should be able to crap
all over society dammit, he's in the NBA! Stop
trying to keep him from feeding his family!" Have
you ever heard a rich athlete say that – "I can't
let them take food out of my family's mouth!"
They make millions of dollars and they have the
audacity to say that to someone with a television

camera. If the NBA did all of this, it would decrease the amount of players getting DUI's, domestic violence issues, drug use, and other reprehensible behavior.

Do Drug Tests Monthly and Randomly. Oh wait, drugs are legal right? No? Not yet? Okay, then do drug tests monthly and randomly! You make millions as a professional athlete, not being part of a rock band. While you are representing a team and a city, it's not unfair to ask of you to live like an athlete and stay away from drugs.

I honestly do not feel that the game or the "system" will change until we get blown out or lose in international play, especially the Olympics. If we do not medal, then people will ask "what is wrong with basketball in the United States?" Until that happens, nothing will change, but doing as I suggest will change the NBA for the better and the way millions feel about it.

CHAPTER 12

THE SOLUTION PART 2

THE NCAA

P ay the players. They make outrageous amounts of money for their schools, compensate them. If the NCAA paid these players something, it would eliminate a majority of the scandals, secret deals, and illegal transactions. You don't have to pay them much but give them enough so they can live at the school without being forced to take bribes.

If you paid the players, you would eliminate a lot of the scumbag in-between guys that broker illegal deals. Do you want to know what's wrong with that? Nothing!

No more One and Done. A player should have to stay in school for at least three years! For every Kevin Durant and Carmelo Anthony, kids that left school after one year, there are many more who made the decision to enter the draft and they are either stuck at the end of a bench or no longer in the league.

The NCAA has rabid fans. There is one contingent of fans that went to a college and they are diehard fans. There is also a contingent of people that didn't go to school or to one of the major college basketball schools who are loyal fans as well. The problem is that there is a section of this fan base that is switching favorite teams from year to year. They are becoming fickle. Business isn't good when it gets fickle. Marketers will term it as brand loyalty. When there isn't brand loyalty, things can go bad for you very quickly.

It's not the fans' fault, though. As soon as they start to identify with players and a style of play, there is an overhaul the following year with a different style of basketball and a different cast. The One and Done is hurting the NCAA because it is bothering a large portion of their fan base.

There need to be stricter rules for coaches that break the rules! This one here may be my biggest frustration. I work with talent that gets into the top programs in the country; believe me when I tell you that many colleges are cheating. Every once in a while when a coach gets caught, he leaves and gets another contract at a different school and the poor school is saddled with the sanctions imposed because of the coach's actions. That doesn't sound like justice to me. Here's what the NCAA should do with these coaches:

- Suspension for one year without pay for a major violation.
- Suspension for one year without pay for a third strike for committing a minor violation.
- Upon completion of the suspension, a two year probation at half the max salary regardless of where the coach is.

That'll teach 'em.

There should also be stricter penalties for switching conferences.

It would be ideal if we could create an independent organization to enforce NCAA rules with more officers and real power. Heck, if you're not going to pay the players, at least pay to keep the boogeymen thugs away from them! Also, provide subpoena power to the enforcement group. It's almost as if a school or coach doesn't want to answer a question, they don't have to. Subpoena their asses!

Players that take benefits should be suspended from all NCAA play and required to wait three years before entering the NBA.

I'm sorry if this sounds a little harsh to you but the game of basketball, in some schools, is so corrupt that we need to flush out the bad people. Asking them nicely to stop isn't working.

Jay Bilas wrote a great book on how to improve the collegiate game. This was just a quick rundown of my thoughts on how to fix it. If you'd like more information on the subject, please read Jay's book.

Now to address the big elephant in the room: How to fix the AAU?

Parents – don't put your children in AAU teams.

Players – don't play AAU basketball.

Eliminate the current state of the AAU as it exists today. Have NCAA certified camps all across the country, develop the players, and play games there. If you don't know where to find a good camp, reach out to me and I'll tell you!

Were you expecting more?

Millions of kids and their parents were expecting more from AAU basketball too.

CPSIA information can be obtained
at www.ICGtesting.com
Printed in the USA
FFOW04n0357080115
10146FF